A JOURNEY THROUGH HISTORY
THE STORY OF ANCIENT WEAPONS

WILL FOWLER

New York

CONTENTS

This edition published in 2011 by:

The Rosen Publishing Group, Inc.
29 East 21st Street
New York, NY 10010

Additional end matter copyright © 2011 by The Rosen Publishing Group, Inc.

Library of Congress Cataloging-in-Publication Data

Fowler, Will, 1947–
The story of ancient weapons / Will Fowler.
    p. cm. — (A journey through history)
Includes bibliographical references and index.
ISBN 978-1-4488-0623-2 (library binding)
1. Weapons, Ancient—Juvenile literature. 2. Military art and science—History—To 500—Juvenile literature. I. Title.
U805.F69 2011
623.4'41—dc22
                                                    2010005288

Manufactured in the United States of America

CPSIA Compliance Information: Batch #S10YA: For further information, contact Rosen Publishing, New York, New York, at 1-800-237-9932.

Copyright in design, text and images © 1999, 2008 Anness Publishing Limited, U.K.
Previously published as *Exploring History: Ancient Weapons*

Picture Credits

Mark Beesley; Vanessa Card; Rob Chapman (Linden Artists); Wayne Ford; Terry Gabbey; Sally Holmes; Steve Lings (Linden Artists); Kevin Maddison; Terry Riley; Eric Rowe (Linden Artists); Mike Sanders; Peter Sarson; Rob Sheffield; Roger Stewart; Ken Stott; Mike White (Temple Rogers); John Woodcock.
Maps: Stuart Squires and Steve Sweet (SGA).

Page 9 (T/L) Erich Lessing/AKG London; 16 (B/L) E.T. Archive; 24 (T/R) AKG London; 32 (B/R) British Museum/E.T. Archive; 34 (T/R) E.T. Archive; 47 (B/L) Mary Evans Picture Library; 53 (T/R) E.T. Archive; 57 (T/R) Mary Evans Picture Library; 57 (B/L) Mary Evans Picture Library; 59 (B/L) E.T. Archive; 61 (T/R) Mary Evans Picture Library. All other photographs from Dover Publications and Miles Kelly archives.

Introduction

THE USE OF WEAPONS is almost as ancient as humanity. Many early weapons came from hunting tools such as spears and bows, but probably the oldest and most useful weapon is the knife or dagger. A flint dagger from Scandinavia and dated around 1800 BCE is one of the earliest examples found in Europe, but daggers have been made from stone, bone, wood, metal and plastic. Today, soldiers are armed with bayonets or combat knives, weapons whose origins can be traced back to the simple dagger.

The development of weaponry and warfare runs alongside the development of early civilizations. As Stone Age people moved out of caves and simple shelters, they banded together to form tribes and clans and built villages. Bronze replaced stone and flint for tools, and then iron replaced bronze. People began to acquire valuable possessions such as food stocks and animals, agricultural equipment, clothing and cooking utensils, and finally precious and attractive adornments and decorations. For the first time, weapons were needed, not just for hunting, but for self-defense and attack against other humans. The horses, which herdsmen used to move cattle, also allowed armed warriors to travel farther and faster than people on foot. Raids and ambushes by horsemen, as well as movements by nomadic mounted tribes, became part of daily life.

▲ ARMOR
This Japanese warrior wears armor made from bamboo wood. Today, armor is made from plastic or nylon.

▼ KEY DATES
The panel charts the progress of weapons and warfare from the Stone Age to the 1600s.

▼ FORTIFICATIONS
Legionaries patrol Hadrian's Wall. Once territory had been won or taken, rulers needed to defend their lands or empires. Castles and walls guarded by troops were built all over Europe.

THE FIRST WEAPONS

10,000–5000 BCE Cave paintings in Spain show men armed with bows in combat.

3500 BCE The Royal Standard of Ur, Sumerian pictures made from shells and precious stones, shows men armed with clubs, axes and spears.

2500 BCE First fortified city, Ur of the Chaldees in Modern Iraq.

1680 BCE The Hyksos introduce horse-drawn chariots to Egypt.

Assyrian siege towers

1800 BCE Flint daggers made in Sweden.

Hittite chariot

1600 BCE Bronze weapons in Sweden and Greece.

1469 BCE The first record of a battle, at Megiddo, between Egypt and the Canaanites.

1000 BCE Assyrians make use of iron for weapons.

500 BCE In China, Sun Tzu writes the first book on military theory.

GREEKS AND ROMANS

Mediterranean galley

490 BCE The Battle of Marathon fought between the Greeks and the Persians. Both army and navy are used and the Greeks defeat an enemy once thought to be unbeatable.

401 BCE Battle of Cunaxa between Greeks and Persians uses chariots with scythes near Babylon. The Persians won.

387 BCE First siege of Rome by Gauls. The City is burned, but the government buildings remain.

327 BCE Alexander the Great crosses the river Hydaspes and defeats the Indian king Porus.

216 BCE Hannibal of Carthage uses elephants at the Battle of Cannae against the Romans. It was his greatest victory.

206 BCE–CE 220 Cross bows widely used in China.

CE 408–410 The Goths under Alaric besiege Rome and sack it on August 24, 410.

Roman legionary

To reduce the chance of death or injury, men used shields and armor, made from toughened animal hide, wood or wood strengthened with metal. This ancient equipment forms a model for the plastic shields used by modern-day police to protect themselves from the oldest of weapons—the thrown stone. The breastplates worn by ancient cavalries are copied by the "flak jackets" worn by many soldiers and helicopter crews today.

Tribal raids to steal goods or settle territorial disputes led to the building of fortifications. The fences and ditches built to control wild or domesticated animals were just as effective against raiding parties. Wood was easy to get and to work with, but could be set on fire by attackers, and would rot in time. Stone or mud brick was tougher and more enduring. Today, fortifications may no longer be towering castles, but we still use sandbag parapets, trenches and bunkers.

Ancient weapons relied for their effectiveness on human or animal strength although heavy shields and armor made maneuvring awkward. Warfare stayed much the same until the late 1800s when the internal combustion engine was invented.

▲ ANIMALS
Before the invention of the combustion engine, animals— usually horses—were used to transport troops, weapons and supplies. In the Crusades in the Middle Ages, both European knights and Saracen warriors fought on horseback. A medieval knight wore such heavy armor that he had to be lifted onto his horse by crane.

▼ TECHNOLOGY
Gunpowder was probably invented in China in the 10th century. The Arabs made the first known guns in about 1300. From the 1400s, muskets were developed in Europe and were gradually improved to allow them to be carried into battle.

VIKINGS TO THE MIDDLE AGES

500 Saxon raids on Britain from north Germany.

778 Battle of Roncesvalles. The Franks under Charlemagne beaten by Basques and Gascons.

700s to 1000s Norse raids on Britain and Europe.

The Norman conquest

1066 The Battle of Hastings. William of Normandy invades Britain and seizes power.

1095–99 The First Crusade. European Christian armies fight for the Holy Land.

1120 Welsh archers use long bows for the first time at Powys.

1190 Mongols under Genghis Khan begin expansion south and west from the Gobi Desert.

1330 First steel produced by accident in the Middle East while making iron.

1326 First illustration of cannon appears in manuscripts in Europe.

1337 Hundred Years War between England and France begins.
Medieval cannon

GUNPOWDER AND AFTER

1400 Handguns first produced in Europe. *Hand cannon*

1400–1600 Rise of halberdiers and pikemen in Europe. Simple breech loading guns in use.

1411 Earliest illustration of a simple matchlock.

1415 Battle of Agincourt. The last great victory of the longbow.

1420s Jan Zizka and the Hussites pioneer the use of war wagons and shoulder-fired guns.

1453 Massed artillery used by Turks at the Siege of Constantinople.

1500 Metal shot gains widespread use.

1505 First battleworthy pistol developed in Germany.

1547 Flintlocks developed in Spain.

1595 English begin to use firearms and cannon.

1635 Flintlocks perfected in France.

1620 Swedes first use light leather-bound cannon. First tactical use of artillery.

Clubs, Maces, Hammers and Flails

THE EARLIEST KIND of weapons were clubs, maces and hammers. People could hold them in their hands. They could not break down and nothing could go wrong with them. The club is the oldest weapon. The earliest clubs were lumps of stone picked up from the ground. Prehistoric people used them as both tools and weapons. Clubs could be used to crush up seeds for food. They could be used as weapons to hunt animals or to fight with enemies. In South Africa, there are wall paintings made around 6000 BCE showing two human figures with long heavy sticks that look like clubs. People also made clubs from long, heavy animal bones or thick lengths of wood taken from trees, bushes or plants.

When people learned how to make bronze, iron and steel, they used these metals to make stronger weapons. Using metal, the simple club was turned into a mace. A mace had a weighted, spiked or pointed end. This could be used to batter through an enemy's

▲ CLUBS AND MACES AT HASTINGS
The Bayeux tapestry showing Norman cavalry, armed with maces and clubs, at the Battle of Hastings in 1066.

▲ THE MACE
This elaborately crafted mace is a weapon of war but may also serve as a symbol of political or military status.

shield or armor. It could be used in hand-to-hand fighting or by soldiers on horseback. Today in the US a ceremonial mace, made of ebony and silver, is used in the House of Representatives. In Britain, the scepter carried by the queen on special occasions is also a kind of mace.

The war hammer was like an ordinary carpenter's claw hammer, but had only one claw. This was a kind of spiked pick. The shaft, or handle, of a war hammer was up to 3.3 feet (or 1 meter) in length. A soldier using a hammer could reach out from his saddle to strike his enemy. Using the sharp claw of the hammer, the soldier could then puncture his enemy's metal helmet. This kind of blow to the head could be fatal, killing instantly.

The flail was first used by farmers to thresh corn. It was made into a weapon which is a mixture of mace and club. Between one and three lengths of chain were fixed to one end of a thick metal stick. Weighted spikes were attached to the end of each length of chain. When the flail was used, the chains whipped through the air, and struck the enemy in several places at once.

SIMPLE WEAPONS FOR CLOSE COMBAT

In its most primitive form, a club or contact weapon extends the reach of a person in close combat and replaces their feet or fists as weapons. It can be made from any spare wood or timber. Later the use of metal and the positioning of the weight at one end made these contact weapons much more effective in battle.

◀ THE SHILLELAGH
This Irish chieftain holds a shillelagh, a type of club made from hard wood like blackthorn or oak. Clubs are the simplest of contact weapons. In a more sophisticated version, they are still used today in the form of police night sticks.

African club

South Sea Island club

New Zealand club

▲ CLUBS FROM ACROSS THE WORLD
Clubs made from wood, bone and stone with both ritual and warlike functions can be found throughout the world. Some combine two materials, so a wooden haft may be weighted with stone. Another method is to pour molten lead into a hole made in the top of the club. Leather strips may be added to the handle to improve grip, or a loop for the user's wrist.

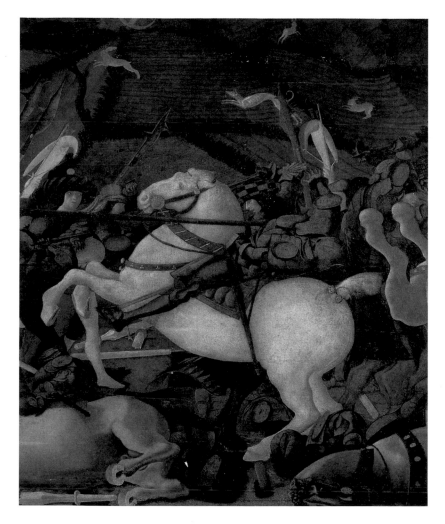

◄ THE ROUT OF SAN ROMANO
*This detail from a painting by the Italian
Renaissance artist Uccello shows armor-clad
horsemen wielding maces, hammers and bows.*

▲ HAMMER VERSUS MACE
*Even though medieval knights wore complicated
armor, they still fought with simple weapons.
In this picture you can see how the hammer and
mace were used, and how powerful they look.*

16th-century war hammer

▲ WAR HAMMER
*The spike on the war hammer was designed
to penetrate armor. The flat end was used
for smashing in helmets.*

16th-century Polish mace

15th-century English mace

15th-century spiked mace

15th-century morning star mace

◄ MACES AND MORNING STARS
The mace was in effect a metal club. The
morning star was derived from the
hinged agricultural flail, used to beat
corn. Both came in a variety of styles.
Some of them had deadly spikes or
heavy blunt ends.

▶ DEATH STAR
This knight prepares to deliver a lethal blow
with his morning star. The name came from
the spiked metal ball on the end of the chain.
It was said to look like the twinkling
morning star as it sliced through the air.

Key Dates

- 6000 BCE Cave paintings of
  first clubs in Africa.

- CE 1066 Bishop Odo and
  William I carry maces at
  the Battle of Hastings.

- 1200–1600 Morning stars,
  maces, war hammers
  employed in battle.

- 1856 Truncheons used by
  police in Great Britain.

- 1914–1918 Clubs used in
  trench raids during World
  War I. They were used at
  night when silence and
  stealth were vital.

Axes and Throwing Weapons

The ax was first used as a woodsman's tool for felling trees. The first axes, like the first clubs, were made from sharp stones or flints. They were simply cutting tools. Later they were fixed to shafts or handles, which made them more powerful. They could be swung first to put more force behind the blow.

Axes were first made by tying sharp flints into forked or split branches. When people learned how to use bronze, iron and steel, they made stronger, sharper axes. By the time of the Iron Age, ax heads could be cast with a socket to fit the handle. Then, the blade was hammered and ground to a sharp edge. Axes are still made in the same way today.

Axes have always been symbols used by powerful kings and rulers. The double-headed bronze ax was used as the symbol of the Minoan civilization in Crete. Pictures of the ax were used in wall paintings and as decoration on pottery.

The hand ax had a short handle. It could be used to hack the enemy in hand-to-hand combat. Soldiers could also throw the ax, although this meant they might lose it. A

▲ DECORATIVE AX HEADS
The simple wedge shape of an ax head has often been decorated for war or ritual throughout the world.

◀ KNIGHT WITH AX
Medieval knights often rode into battle armed with a heavy battle-ax. This had a sharp blade and a spike. The ax was attached to the knight's arm with a chain. These axes could cause terrible injuries to both men and horses.

good example of a fighting ax was the tomahawk used by Native North Americans. Tomahawks were first made of stone, then later of steel brought by traders. They were used for hunting and fighting. The tomahawk had a long handle which gave it a powerful swing. British soldiers fighting in North America in the 18th century adopted the tomahawk for their own use.

The last time an ax was used in combat in Europe was at the battle of Waterloo in 1815 between the French and the British, together with the Prussians. During the battle, French troops used axes to break

THROWING WEAPONS
The simplest hand-thrown weapon is the sharp-edged stone. However, metal and wood are more effective. The Franks of the 5th and 6th century used an iron throwing ax called a Francisca. Native North Americans used the tomahawk up to the 19th century.

◀ CHAKRAM
The Sikhs of India used a razor-sharp steel war-quoit or chakram, which they used to throw at the enemy. Chakrams were in use as late as the 19th century.

Chakram

Australian boomerangs

◀ BOOMERANGS
War boomerangs do not return to the thrower, unlike the hunting version. Their sharp edges wound or stun the opposition.

▼ NORSE RAIDERS
Norse raiders disembark from their longships and race into action armed with their single-headed war axes. These iron-bladed weapons were often elaborately decorated.

down the door of the farm at Hougoument, which was being held by the British infantry.

The ax is still in use today. In some armies, it is the badge of the assault pioneers. These are soldiers who do engineering work. The badge shows crossed axes. Firefighters also use axes which look rather like ancient war axes. They have spikes and blades and are easy to hold and use in one hand.

▼ THROWING KNIFE
The leaf-shaped throwing knife was a war weapon used throughout Africa from Nigeria through the Congo to the Sudan. As it turned through the air in flight, the blades of the throwing knife were intended to strike the victim in a sawing action. The disadvantage of a throwing weapon was that if it missed, it could be thrown back.

African throwing knife

◄ WAR BLADE
This African throwing knife had a steel, double-edged blade. The short handle was bound with grass or a leather thong to give the warrior a good grip. The knife was designed purely as a weapon, unlike an everyday knife, and could not be used off the battlefield for day-to-day tasks or hunting.

Key Dates

- 2000–1700 BCE Double-headed ax used as symbol for the civilization of Minoan Crete.

- 700 BCE Evidence that slings were used in Assyria.

- CE 400–500 Francisca throwing axes found in England.

- 700–1100 Single- and double-bladed axes used by Norse raiders.

- 900–1400 Heavy, long-handled battle-axes used by knights.

- 1700s Iron-bladed tomahawks manufactured for North America.

- 1800s Chakrams in use in India.

Slings, Bows and Crossbows

The sling, like the longbow and crossbow, is a "stand-off" weapon. This lets a soldier attack his enemy while remaining out of reach himself. Slings were used in early sea battles. Piles of sling stones were discovered at Maiden Castle, Dorset, where the Celtic defenders fought the Romans in CE 44.

Bows are among the most ancient weapons in the world. Ancient cave paintings, dating from 10,000 and 5000 BCE, from Castellon in Spain show figures of men using bows for fighting. Bows have been found in Denmark dating from 2000 to 1500 BCE and in Egypt from around 1400 BCE.

Though the bow was used in war, it was also used for hunting. Many of the skills of the hunter were also those of the warrior. Experienced archers could fire accurately from horseback or chariot.

In the 16th century, Henry VIII of England ordered that young men should practice shooting their bows every Sunday after the morning service at church. Most bows were made from yew wood.

The triumph of the English and Welsh longbow was in three battles against France: Crécy on August 26, 1346; Poitiers on September 19, 1356; and Agincourt on October 25, 1415. English and Welsh archers were able to keep the French mounted nobles under a constant rain of arrows from 800 feet (244 meters). As horses and riders crashed to the ground, others became entangled with them and they all became easy targets.

When muskets and rifles were first invented, the longbow, in the hands of a skilled archer, was still more accurate. It was not until the American Civil War of 1861–65 that firearms became more effective. Muskets were adopted by armies simply because it was easier to train soldiers to use them.

Some armies used men armed with crossbows. The crossbow is a short bow attached to a piece of wood or

▲ DAVID AND THE GIANT GOLIATH
The shepherd David defeated the Philistine warrior Goliath by stunning him with a sling stone.

◀ TAKING AIM
A crossbowman takes aim. He operated the trigger, which held back the string with a hook called a nut, with his right hand. If the weapon was used to hunt game, a stone was used in place of the bolt.

◀ TAKING COVER
A crossbowman takes cover with his weapon and equipment stowed in a shield carrier.

STAND OFF WEAPONS

The crossbow and longbow allowed ordinary foot soldiers to engage enemies at long range. This meant that mounted knights and foot soldiers could be killed before they could use their swords, lances or axes. Both longbows and crossbows could penetrate armor at short range, which meant that they could bring down a knight in full armor.

Longbow with six arrows   Longbow   Range of 245 yards (224 meters)

Crossbow with one bolt   Crossbow   Range of 390 yards (357 meters)

Using the Crossbow

Spanning

Fitting the bolt

Taking aim

▲ SHOOTING RANGE
The expert longbowman could fire up to six aimed arrows in a minute to a range of about 245 yards (224 m), or twelve less accurately. On the other hand, the skilled crossbowman had a longer range at 390 yards (357 m), but a far slower rate of fire. He could only shoot one bolt a minute.

▲ THREE STAGES
It took much longer to load a crossbow than to aim and fire an arrow. There were three stages to loading and firing a crossbow. Spanning was the first stage. It involved pulling the bow string back and locking it. Then the bolt was fitted into the slot. Finally the bow was aimed and fired. With mechanical assistance as many as four bolts could be fired in a minute.

▼ LONGBOWS IN ACTION
*English and Welsh longbowmen
protected by a palisade of stakes fire
at advancing French knights.*

metal called a stock. The bowstring was pulled back by hand or mechanically and held in place by a hook and trigger mechanism. The short arrow, or bolt, was fitted into a slot and aligned with the string. The crossbowman had only to aim and operate the trigger.

The first description of a crossbow appears in a book called *The Art of War* by the Chinese military thinker Sun Tzu, writing in 500 BCE. In 1139, Pope Innocent II tried to ban the use of the crossbow against Christians because of the terrible injuries it caused. Richard I of England died in 1199 from gangrene caused by a crossbow bolt.

Forked steel
tip

Barbed
arrowhead

▲ ARROWHEADS
Archers used different shaped arrowheads. Barbs and forks were popular. Barbs ensured that the arrow stayed lodged in the target and made withdrawal difficult. The forked steel tip was used in the Far East.

Horse
Foot
Archers   Tramecourt
Foot   Archers
Archers
Archers
Agincourt
Archers
N
Archers   Foot
Archers
Foot
Road to
Calais
Village
Maisoncelles
English
French

◄ LONGBOWS SAVE THE DAY
The Battle of Agincourt was the last great victory of the longbow against mounted soldiers. Wet weather slowed down the French knights, and the English and Welsh archers stopped two attacks before Henry V's forces attacked from the rear. The French were defeated and lost about 5,000 of their men.

Key Dates

- 10,000–5000 BCE Cave paintings in Spain show archers in battle.

- 500 BCE Sun Tzu writing about military doctrine mentions crossbows.

- CE 1100 Crossbows widely used in Europe.

- 1199 King Richard I of England killed by a crossbow at Chaluz in France.

- 1200s Longbow enters wide use in England and Wales.

- 1914–1918 Crossbows used for firing grenades in the trench warfare during World War I.

Daggers and Knives

SMALL, LIGHT AND EASY TO CARRY, daggers and knives are hand-held weapons. Daggers and knives make very good secret weapons as they can be used in complete silence. They were used on their own for hand-to-hand fighting, or for throwing.

Although the dagger design was based on the knife, there is an important difference between the two. The knife is a simple tool, sharp along one edge of the blade, it may have a relatively blunt point. It can be used for everyday tasks like cutting up meat for example, as well as being used as a weapon. A dagger, is double-edged and tapers along its length to a sharp point. It may have a guard between the blade and the handle to protect the user's hand. It is always classified as a weapon.

The earliest daggers were made from flint. Early daggers were also made from sharpened wood or bone. Daggers made from bronze, iron and steel lasted longer.

◀ SWORD AND DAGGER
A fully armored knight equipped with a sword and dagger. The sword was suitable for hacking and the dagger for thrusts to gaps in the armor.

▶ MURDER WEAPON
Lurking in the shadows, an assassin armed with a stiletto awaits his victim. This dagger was easy to conceal and deadly if it penetrated a vital organ.

Stiletto

DAGGER DESIGN

As a weapon, a dagger or knife was inexpensive and very effective in even unskilled hands. It could be used for agricultural or domestic work if necessary. A dagger consists of the blade, the cross guard that protects the user's hand and knuckles, the grip or handle and the pommel. In a fight, the pommel at the base of the grip could be used in the same way as a hammer on an opponent's head. Dagger designs vary from country to country. The Indian katar or push dagger was designed to be used in a punching action.

Pommel

Grip or handle

Blade

◀ A BLADE FROM THE BRONZE AGE
This Swedish dagger dates from around 1350–1200 BCE and shows all the basic design principles of a hand-held edged weapon. It has a separate riveted hilt, distinct pommel and double-edged blade with fullers or blood grooves. Later designs would have a full-length tang, an extension of the blade, built into the handle. This gave the dagger greater strength and better balance.

Malay creese

Central African dagger

Indian curved dagger

Moorish dagger

Indian katar

▶ A DUEL
Duels were considered an honorable way to settle an argument. The stiletto is used here to block the sword thrust.

In the 14th and 15th centuries, sword fighters used daggers with their swords. A swordsman would hold the dagger in his left hand to block and deflect his enemy's sword. He would then make a thrust with the sword in his right hand.

Swordsmiths were the people who made swords and daggers. The daggers they made were almost works of art. They had beautiful inlays and precious and semi-precious metals and jewels set in the handles. In the Middle Ages, the Saracens of Damascus in Syria developed a method of hammering layers of steel together. This made blades of swords and daggers very hard and sharp and created a pattern rather like watered silk, known as Damascene.

In the 20th century, the dagger and the knife are still used by soldiers in combat. In World War I, the US Army was issued with the Fighting Knife Mk 1, which protected the user's knuckles with a guard that could be used as a "knuckle duster." Modern combat knives are more like multi-purpose tools, with a saw edge, screwdriver and wire cutter as well as a sharp knife blade.

▲ TOLEDO, CITY OF STEEL
This Spanish city was a center for beautifully designed swords, daggers and armor, which were manufactured for many centuries and exported through Europe.

▶ SWORDBREAKER
A 17th-century Italian swordbreaker was a dagger made for special use in a sword fight. It was designed to trap an opponent's sword thrust in its notched blade. The dagger would not be used just to parry a sword thrust. A vigorous twist of the wrist could either break the thin blade of the trapped sword, or wrench it from the user's hands.

Cross guard

Notched blade

Key Dates

- 2000 BCE Bronze daggers were manufactured throughout Europe.

- 500 BCE First Iron Age weapons produced and used widely.

- CE 1600s–1700s Stiletto manufactured in Italy. It was copied and used throughout Europe.

- 1700s–1900s Dress daggers worn as part of military or political uniforms.

- 1820s Bowie knife invented in US by Jim Bowie. Its classic design forms the model for most modern sheath knives.

- 1940s–1990s Combat knives issued to soldiers as multi-function tools.

Swords, Sabers and Scimitars

ONE OF THE MOST ANCIENT weapons in the world, the sword is now a symbol of rank for officers on ceremonial parades. Tools shaped like swords were used in farming work and to cut down trees. Like other working tools, they were adapted to use in fighting. The kukri from Nepal is an ancient weapon that remains in service today with Gurkha regiments of the British army. Its broad, curved blade is ideal for chopping and even digging, but it is also a very good weapon for close combat.

Early swords were used to slice rather than to thrust. For many centuries European swords had a short, straight blade which tapered to a point. It was sharp on both edges. They were first made in bronze, later iron and finally steel. The short Roman steel sword called a gladius was about 20 inches (50 cm) long. It was like a long, wide-bladed dagger. The gladiators who fought in the Roman circus or arena with these swords got their name from the gladius.

Swords in the Middle Ages were longer. They were about 31 to 35 inches (80 to 90 cm) long with a cross-shaped handle and tapering blade. Long swords could be used to thrust at the enemy, but most soldiers fought by hacking at each other. Swords could be used by soldiers on foot or horseback.

Very strong men used the two-handed sword, which was very long, with a broad blade. Swordsmen used both hands to fight with it. Scottish chieftains in the mid-16th century used a long, double-edged, two-handed sword called the claidheamh múr, or claymore. Knights and soldiers discovered the sword-making techniques of the Middle East during the crusades. This led to

▲ VIKING WEAPON
A Viking sword from the 10th century. Its hilt is covered with silver leaf.

◀ TWO-HANDED
Medieval knights in close combat. One of them is armed with a hand-and-a-half, or two-handed sword.

▲ SWORD SKILLS
A Japanese samurai warrior from the 15th century. Samurai warriors usually wore two swords and a distinctive headdress.

SWORDS
Swords today are made from steel and have been made from bronze, stone and even wood. Although no longer used in war, in many cultures they remain the symbol of power and status within military organizations. Sword fighting techniques vary according to the design of the blade. The Japanese favor a chopping action, while the thin-bladed rapier is best suited to a thrust.

▶ SAMURAI WEAPON
The Japanese traditionally used single-edged daggers and swords of different lengths. The traditional long-bladed sword is called a katana.

◀ EASTERN SWORD BLADES
Swords with curved blades came from the Middle East and India. They were lighter and easier to use with one hand than western swords. Soldiers from the west came across them when they fought in the crusades. Curved swords are called sabers or scimitars. This elegant saber was designed in Venice. The saber became popular with mounted troops who could use it against soldiers on foot or on horseback.

◀ DEATH AT DAWN
A Victorian print shows the victor of a duel armed with a rapier. His victim's weapon shows the guard or side rings designed to protect the hand.

▶ HEAVY BLADE
An Asian warrior armed with a bow and broad-bladed sword. The sword has the weight closer to the tip, which makes it ideal for a chopping action.

improved sword design in the west. Soldiers in the Middle East used a curved sword called a scimitar. These had long, narrow blades and very sharp edges.

The guard in front of the sword handle was made to protect the fighter's hand. Around 1600, Venetian sword makers produced a new guard design called the basket hilt. This was a curved, perforated guard that protected the whole hand. The basic design is still used today on many modern ceremonial swords.

The mounted soldiers of the cavalry charged towards their enemy with their swords pointing forward for a straight thrust. However, long swords became difficult to use once the soldiers were fighting close to each other. There was no room to make a good stroke. The saber was developed as a cavalry weapon. It had a short, curved blade and was used to slash and thrust. The blade cut as it went up and as it came down.

In Renaissance Europe, noblemen and courtiers wore weapons almost as fashion accessories. Rapiers were very popular. These were light, very narrow swords with elaborate guards. The fashion lasted from about 1530 through to 1780.

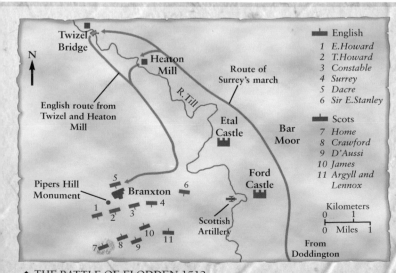

▲ THE BATTLE OF FLODDEN 1513
This battle, between the English and the Scots, took place in Northern England. The Scots fought with the two-handed claymore sword.

Key Dates

- 1300 BCE Bronze swords used in war.
- 650–500 BCE Iron swords in use.
- CE 900s Viking double-edged swords used in Viking raids all over Europe.
- 1300s Curved Turkish sabers in use as a cavalry weapon.
- 1500s Rapiers in use.
- 1500s Scottish two-edged swords in use.
- 1600s Venetian basket-hilt swords in use throughout Europe.
- 1850 Kukri in use with Nepalese soldiers.

Spears, Poles, Pikes and Halberds

PREHISTORIC HUNTERS used spears to kill animals for food. They were more powerful and accurate than simple stones and could be thrown from safe distances. The earliest spears were simply straight saplings (very young trees) which were sharpened at one end. In the Far East, bamboo wood was used. It was light and strong and could be hardened in a fire to give a very sharp point. Flint, stone or metal points fixed on to a spear made it even more effective.

There were soldiers armed with spears in most ancient armies. Another name for the throwing spear is javelin. Throwing spears have one drawback. Once they

▲ THE QUARTERSTAFF
This was the simplest weapon ever made. It could be cut from saplings. In Europe in the Middle Ages, the staff was used more in competitions and brawls than in war.

have been thrown at the enemy, you cannot get them back. In fact, the enemy may use them to throw at you. The Romans solved this problem by inventing a spear called a pilum. This had a long, thin neck near the point. When the spear hit a target, it snapped at the neck. Then it could not be used by the enemy.

Longer, heavier stick weapons were used to fight with rather than to throw. In medieval times, country people used large sticks called staffs for walking. Various types of blades were attached to these to make weapons for both cavalry and infantry troops. A spear point would make a lance, used by cavalry. Knife blades

▶ PIKE WALL
Pikemen in the 17th century lined up to form a barrier for cavalry. This tactic gave musketeers time and space to reload their weapons behind the pike wall.

POLE ARMS
The advantage of pole arms like spears, pikes or halberds is that the user can stab, chop or even entangle his enemy at a safe distance. Peasants often fitted a pruning bill to the shaft of a quarterstaff to make simple pole weapons during revolts and insurrections.

◀ PIKEMAN
A pikeman in the splendid uniform of the 17th century. In addition to his helmet, he might also have a breastplate for extra protection. Pikes had been used as early as 350 BCE, when the Macedonians had pikes nearly 16 feet (5 m) long.

English halberd

Bill

Italian linstock

German glaive

English gisarme

and axes were also used, as well as billhooks, which were tools for cutting hedges. A trident was made by attaching a sharp-pointed fork (like a pitchfork). Halberds were long poles with a spear point and an ax head mounted behind it. Pikes were long, heavy pole weapons with long blades of various designs.

In the 14th and 15th centuries, the Swiss developed specialized pike tactics. Using a pike that consisted of a 20 feet (6 m) shaft and a 3-foot (1 m) iron shank, Swiss soldiers marched in columns which had a front line of 30 men but could be 50 to 100 men deep. The massed pikes could stop a cavalry attack. Many rulers and generals hired Swiss pikemen to fight in their battles. Today, the Pope's Swiss Guard, armed with pikes, is all that is left of this force.

The bayonet fitted to the muzzle of modern army rifles is based on the pike. Bayonets were first used by soldiers with muskets. Although muskets were effective firearms, they took time to reload. By fitting long pointed blades, called bayonets, to their muskets and forming themselves into a hollow square with bayonets pointing outward, soldiers could break up a cavalry attack and protect each other while they reloaded.

◀ SWISS GUARD
The Swiss Guard at the Vatican still carry pikes and wear uniforms similar to those worn in the 15th and 16th centuries.

▶ CLOSE COMBAT
Two soldiers fighting with halberds. One tries to use the curved beak to trip his enemy while the other uses the spike as a spear.

▶ ON THE MOVE
An Etruscan warrior armed with a sword and throwing spear. The classic tactic for these lightly-armed men was to throw their spears, then to run forward as the spears were in flight. By the time the spears reached their target, the Etruscan soldier was within sword reach. The enemy was hit twice in one move.

▲ ISLAND WEAPONS
Spears have been used throughout history in many different cultures. This islander from New Caledonia in the Pacific Ocean is ready to throw one spear and holds two more in reserve.

Key Dates

- 600 BCE Greek hoplites use short throwing spears.

- 350 BCE The sarissa (light spear) used in Macedonian phalanx formations.

- 200–100 BCE Roman foot soldiers use the pilum, or heavy javelin.

- CE 900–1400 Lances used by knights for jousting and war in Europe.

- 1400s Pole ax enters service.

- 1400–1599 Halberd widely used.

- 1600s Pikes enter service.

- 1815 Cavalry lances adopted by Britain from France.

Ancient Firearms

FIREARMS ARE WEAPONS that use gunpowder and shot. The earliest firearms in the west were made around the beginning of the 15th century. They worked rather like mini cannons and were small enough to be carried by a soldier on foot or on horseback. They looked rather like the modern hand-held flare used to signal an emergency at sea. They had a short barrel attached to a handle.

By the late 15th and early 16th centuries, the standard firearm was about 5 feet (1.5 m) long with a barrel, stock and butt. The stock supported the metal barrel and the butt rested in the crook of the firer's shoulder when the gun was being used.

The arquebus was a bigger weapon, often used mounted on a simple tripod. It usually needed two people to operate it. One aimed it and the second put a lit taper into the touch hole or vent.

The soldiers who had to carry these heavy weapons were very keen for craftsmen to make them lighter and easier firearms. The matchlock was the first improvement. This weapon was fired using a fuse or length of cord which had been soaked in a chemical called saltpeter. This made it burn slowly. The cord was coiled into a curved lever called a serpent. A shallow pan filled with gunpowder had a thin tube leading into the barrel of the weapon. To operate the matchlock, the soldier lit the cord, opened the spring-loaded cover to the pan and then pulled the trigger. This brought the burning

▲ MATCHLOCK
The matchlock was used in Europe until the 18th century and in parts of India until as late as the 20th century.

▶ MOUNTED FIREPOWER
The wheel lock was ideal for mounted soldiers who would need to keep one hand free.

HANDGUNS
Improved metal technology and designs made handguns more reliable and easier to carry. Tactics for infantry and cavalry changed to suit these firearms. Weapons were still made by craftsmen. After the Napoleonic wars, muskets and guns began to be mass produced.

▲ POWDER HORN
Gunpowder was stored in a powder horn to keep it dry. Many of them were made from hollow animal horns. They had a spout through which an exact measure of powder was dispensed.

▶ HAND MADE
The lead ball fired by muskets was easily made using a simple mold. Once the molten lead had hardened, the handles of the mold were opened and the new ammunition was ready. Soldiers made their own ammunition as needed.

Mold

Shot

Inside a rifled gun barrel

Bullet spinning from the barrel

▲ RIFLING
Rifling was a system of grooves inside the barrel of a firearm, which gave the bullet a spin as it left the barrel. This made the gun more accurate. Rifled weapons were still rare in the early 19th century. Now rifling is used in every modern gun.

◀ MUSKETEERS
Musketeers armed with the heavy Spanish-style matchlock weapon that required a fork rest for easy handling. This weapon was used by armies throughout Europe from about 1567 for over 100 years, and the musketeers were an elite within the army.

▶ WHEEL LOCK
This firearm used a spring-loaded wheel and pieces of iron pyrites to produce sparks, which ignited the gunpowder at the moment of firing. But they were expensive and not in common use.

cord, or match, down into gunpowder, which exploded.

The matchlock was not a practical weapon for a soldier mounted on horseback who needed to have one hand on the reins. So the wheel lock was developed. It worked rather like an old-fashioned cigarette lighter. When the trigger was pulled the pan of gunpowder was uncovered. A metal wheel rubbed against a lump of iron pyrites and produced a stream of sparks. A mounted soldier could carry two or three short-

barreled wheel lock pistols in holsters on his saddle or tucked into the tops of his riding boots.

The snaphaunce, miguelet and flintlock were later firearms. They used flint and steel to produce a spark. The flintlock was in use until the mid-19th century. A trained soldier could fire a shot every 20 seconds from a smoothbore flintlock musket, but the weapon was inaccurate beyond 87 yards (80 m).

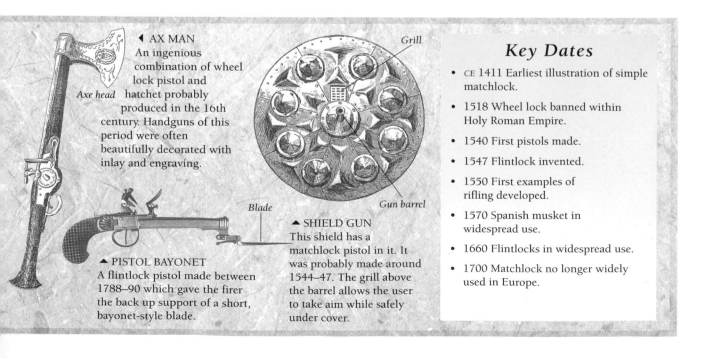

◀ AX MAN
An ingenious combination of wheel lock pistol and hatchet probably produced in the 16th century. Handguns of this period were often beautifully decorated with inlay and engraving.

Axe head

Blade

▲ PISTOL BAYONET
A flintlock pistol made between 1788–90 which gave the firer the back up support of a short, bayonet-style blade.

Grill

Gun barrel

▲ SHIELD GUN
This shield has a matchlock pistol in it. It was probably made around 1544–47. The grill above the barrel allows the user to take aim while safely under cover.

Key Dates

- CE 1411 Earliest illustration of simple matchlock.

- 1518 Wheel lock banned within Holy Roman Empire.

- 1540 First pistols made.

- 1547 Flintlock invented.

- 1550 First examples of rifling developed.

- 1570 Spanish musket in widespread use.

- 1660 Flintlocks in widespread use.

- 1700 Matchlock no longer widely used in Europe.

Armor

SOLDIERS WORE ARMOR to protect the head, neck, eyes and chest. Early armor was made from bronze. Later iron and steel were used. Japanese warriors wore armor made from bamboo wood. There is a problem with armor. It must be thick or heavy enough to protect the soldier wearing it, but light enough for him to move about easily.

The ancient Greeks were the first to use bronze armor. They used it to protect their forearms, legs and chest. A Roman legionary wore armor which covered his chest, stomach, back and shoulders. This protected his lungs, heart and the important blood vessels in the neck. Although his arms and legs were not protected, he could still move and run quickly and easily.

A cheap way to make armor was to sew metal plates on to a heavily padded tunic. By the time of the Battle of Hastings in 1066, nobles and soldiers wore chain or link mail. It protected them from sword, arrow or spear thrusts. It could also move with their bodies. Mail was made by linking iron rings together

to make a kind of metal fabric. Norman and Saxon soldiers both wore a tunic that covered the arms and body as far as the knees. A hood made from mail covered the head. Underneath ring mail, soldiers wore padded jackets. This stopped the mail being pushed into their skin by the force of a sword thrust.

Plate armor became very popular in medieval Europe. The whole body was covered with plates that were either strapped on to the wearer or hinged off one another. This was called a suit of armor. Each suit was made to fit exactly. Although the metal was heavy, its weight was so well balanced that a knight could walk about in reasonable comfort when wearing it. The parts of the armor that were most likely to be struck by a sword were specially angled so that the sword blade would slide off without doing harm.

▲ ANCIENT ARMOUR
A figure dressed in classical armor of Greece and Rome with a breastplate covering his torso and shinpads called greaves protecting his lower legs.

▲ JAPANESE WARRIOR
Japanese armor consisted of bamboo plates sewn to a padded jacket. Mythical motifs decorated the helmet.

PROTECTION
Chain mail was both light and sword-proof, but was never as strong as plate armor. The answer to this problem, for many centuries, was to use chain mail in areas such as the neck and limb joints and plate armor in slabs on the chest, back, legs and arms. The top of the head was protected by plate armor.

◀ NORMAN MAIL COAT
A Norman soldier wearing chain mail coat and helmet, light and flexible armor made from linked steel rings.

◀ INDIAN MAIL HELMET
This helmet uses a combination of plate and chain or ring mail to protect the head and neck. It is similar to the helmets worn by the Saracens.

▶ SHARK ARMOR
Shark's teeth stitched on to a simple tunic made strong armor for warriors of the Sandwich Islands in the Pacific.

▲ BRIGANDINE
The brigandine was a kind of 16th-century flak jacket. It was a short, flexible coat wit protective rivets on th inside and a rich fabri on the outside.

Simple rivets   Plates

Leather fasteners

◀ ROMAN BREASTPLATE
Roman armor was made of plates held together with bronze hinges. In later versions, these were replaced by simple rivets and strong hooks.

Roman foot soldier

◀ MOUNTED ARMOR
Knights might be well protected, but their horses could easily get hurt in battle. To protect them, they wore their own armor.

The same care and attention that went into making armor for the knight was given to that for his horse. How much armor they both wore and how richly it was decorated, showed the owner's wealth.

This kind of armor was very expensive. Both the knight who owned it and the armorer who made it wanted it to look beautiful as well as to work well. It was engraved and inlaid with metals such as brass and even gold. Enamel was used to color the metal plates so that knights appeared in black, green or even red armor.

Even though plate armor was worn in medieval times, soldiers still used chain mail to protect parts of the body that armor could not cover. Later, cavalry troopers, armed with sabers and ready to engage in hand-to-hand fighting, wore chain mail around their necks to prevent their throats being slashed open.

▶ A SUIT OF ARMOR
Knights had their armor specially made to fit. Armor was made up from lots of separate pieces. It was laced or strapped together and hung off a gorget. This was a metal collar that protected the neck and shoulders. A suit of armor from the 16th century was made up of at least 16 pieces and took a long time to put on. Knights needed a squire to help them get ready for battle. Armor was very heavy, but it was so cleverly made that the knights could still move around fairly easily. Most of the names of the pieces of armor are from the French language.

Close helmet — Visor
— Gorget
Pauldron —
— Cuirass
— Vambrace
— Gauntlet
Cuisse —
— Poleyn
Greave —

Key Dates

- 1500–1200 BCE Bronze Mycenaean armor.
- 460 BCE Corinthian armor.
- 102 BCE Mail armor used by Romans.
- CE 75–100 Roman legionary interlocked plate armor widely used.
- 1100s Norman mail armor.
- 1300s Jointed plate armor.
- 1500s Horse armor widely used.
- 1600s Pikemen's armor.
- 1990s Body armor made from plastic or nylon is used today by police forces and armies.

Shields

BODY ARMOR was part of the wearer's "clothing." A shield was a piece of moveable armor. It was normally carried by or strapped to the left arm, while a weapon was held in the right hand. It could be used to push aside an opponent's sword or spear. Like all armor, a shield has to be strong enough to defend its user yet light enough for him to carry easily. It also has to be made in a shape that will give the user most protection.

The earliest shields were made from animal skin stretched over a wooden frame. They were rather like the shields carried by African warriors in the 18th and 19th centuries.

The first metal shields were made of bronze. The ancient Greeks used large round shields. In ancient Britain, Celtic warriors used round bronze shields and figure-of-eight shaped shields. Circular shields were used by cavalry in both ancient Greece and Rome. Round shields were used later by the cavalry in the armies of the

▲ GREEK PROTECTION
A Greek hoplite of 600 BCE equipped with a round bronze hoplon shield. Bronze was easy to work, but was softer than iron.

▲ RIOT PROTECTION
Modern German police with polycarbonate riot shields and helmets as protection against rocks and petrol bombs in riots.

▼ GALLIC SHIELD
The Norman inverted tear-drop shaped shield covered the torso, but left the legs free.

Middle and Far East. The Vikings also had round shields.

Roman legionaries used an oblong shield that was slightly curved. It was large enough to protect a man from his shoulders to his knees. The shields could fit together. A group of legionaries lined up in rows of four could fit their shields together and form a very strong barrier. Used in this way, the shields made a kind of temporary tank. Well protected, the whole unit moved forwards to attack with their short swords.

SHIELDS

Shields could be used to block a sword blow or protect the head and shoulders from arrows. The Greeks and Romans had finely crafted shields. In medieval times, shields were plainer but made from tougher materials.

◀ INSIGNIA
Knights wore insignia on their shields and armor to identify themselves on the battlefield. Here a simple bar and two dots are repeated, like a brand name, on the knight's shield, lance and the trappings of his horse.

▼ OUT OF AFRICA
The Zulu war shield is made from hardened animal skin on a wooden frame. It is light and tough. The warrior can use it to deflect blows.

▶ CELTIC CRAFT
The bronze Celtic shield is like a Roman design. The metal decoration on the front shows the wealth and position of the shield's owner.

The Romans developed a shield technique for attacking walls and castles. The soldiers fitted their shields together above their heads making what was called a testudo, or tortoise. Once the "tortoise" had reached the walls of the castle, the shields provided a platform for men to climb up to the fortifications.

By the time of the Norman invasion of 1066 shields had changed to a distinctive kite shape. The shield tapered downwards, so the user could move his legs, but protected his upper body. Both cavalry and infantry used this type of shield.

The medieval shields were smaller. English and Welsh archers used a small round shield while knights had shields that were flat along the top edge and tapered to a point. This shape is now the accepted pattern for modern heraldry. It was in this period that shields were painted with the coats-of-arms of their users so they could be recognized by their followers on the battlefield.

▲ THE TOUGH TORTOISE

The Roman interlocked shield pattern called a tortoise allowed troops to approach the enemy fortifications under cover. Soldiers would then climb on their shields to attack the enemy walls.

▲ MOON POWER
The raised symbols of the sun and moon on this Persian shield were meant to give extra power to the user.

▶ ANCIENT PERSIAN SHIELD
This shield from Persia has cut-outs at arm level. These allowed the soldier to attack with his spear while he was still protected by his shield.

◀ BUCKLER SHIELD
This round German shield called a buckler has decorative studs called bosses set in an unusual random pattern.

Key Dates

- 1750-1600 BCE Wood and hide shields used by Mycenaean soldiers.
- 480 BCE Bronze and wood shields used by Athenian hoplites.
- 400 BCE Celtic shield fittings found in England.
- 400 BCE Hide shields replace bronze types for Athenian troops.
- 300 BCE Roman soldiers equipped with hide and wicker shields.
- CE 1000–1200 Norman and Norse troops use tear-drop shields.
- 1400s Shields with coats-of-arms used by knights.

Helmets and War Hats

▲ SAXON HELMET
This helmet from the 7th century comes from the Saxon burial ground at Sutton Hoo. It is inlaid with silvered bronze.

SOLDIERS HAVE ALWAYS worn helmets of some kind to protect their heads and eyes in combat. They came in all shapes and sizes, to suit the kind of weapons soldiers were likely to come up against. Ancient helmets were designed to protect soldiers from attack by cutting weapons such as swords or thrusting weapons such as spears or arrows. Some helmets were simple round metal hats. Others were more like iron masks. The ancient Greeks invented the nosepiece. This was a strip of armor running from the brim of the helmet along the bridge of the nose. It was still in use in the 17th century. The Romans favored helmets with deep cheek pieces. These were hinged flaps that hung down the sides of the helmet, covering the ears and cheeks, but leaving the front unrestricted. This made it easier for the wearer to see clearly as he was fighting.

In the 11th century, the Normans wore conical helmets with nosepieces. They also wore a chain mail hood which completely covered the ears and back of the neck. This gave them added protection.

PROTECTING THE HEAD

Since the head incorporates the brain and face with important organs such as the eyes, ears, nose and mouth, it has always been protected in war. Helmets were made from bronze, iron or steel. Today they are made from modern plastics and polymers, which are light but very strong.

◄ THE GREAT HELM
By the mid-14th century, the helm was the most widely used helmet by mounted knights. A visor pulled down to protect the face. Helms often sported elaborate crests at the top showing the owner's coat-of-arms. Today's motorcycle helmets resemble the helm.

Assyrian war hat

Hoplite helmet

Assyrian helmet

▲ ANCIENT HELMETS
Helmets began as simple metal hats. Later, hinged flaps were added to give protection to the cheeks, nose and neck without making it too difficult for the soldier to see or move. The flaps were often decorated.

◀ SPEED OR STRENGTH
During the crusades of the 11th and 12th centuries, European knights, who wore heavy armor and helmets, met Saracen warriors who wore lighter mail coats and small helmets that fitted close to their heads.

The most magnificent helmets were made during the medieval period in Europe. Ordinary foot soldiers had simple armor including a plain helmet but royalty and noblemen had splendid armor and helmets. The helmets were engraved and inlaid and were made with angles to deflect sword blows and a hinged visor that protected the wearer's eyes. A three-dimensional model of the family crest was often set on top. These elaborate helmets were like badges to show the nobility of the wearer.

By the time of the English Civil War (1642–1651), helmet design had changed. There was neck and earflap protection, a hinged peak and a face guard. The helmet was known as a "lobster-tail pot" because it looked like a lobster shell.

When the helmet was revived in World War I, the British army adopted the style of the brimmed war hat worn by archers at the Battle of Agincourt (1415). It was called the "kettle."

▶ MEDIEVAL HELMETS
Armorers in the Middle Ages produced helmets and armor for wealthy and discriminating customers. Some designs were very fanciful. Others had carefully constructed angles and shapes which could deflect sword or mace blows.

English 13th century

French 15th century

French 12th century

French 13th century

German 15th century

Key Dates

- 1700–1100 BCE Bronze helmets in use in Mycenae.

- 55 BC–CE 100 Roman cavalry and infantry helmets introduced.

- 1000–1100 Norman helmets with nosepiece.

- 1300s Basinet hinged helmet.

- 1350s Helms in use by European knights in battle and in tournaments.

- 1400s Kettle-hat or war hat.

- 1500s Nuremberg close helmets.

- 1600s Pot or lobster-tail pot helmet worn by Cromwell's Roundhead army in the English Civil War.

Animals at War

ELEPHANTS, HORSES, DONKEYS, bullocks and camels have all been used to fight wars. Most of them were used to carry soldiers or pull wagons. Elephants were used rather like modern tanks. An elephant could trample enemy soldiers, while archers riding in a large basket on its back could pick off targets with their arrows.

▼ HANNIBAL'S TANKS
The most famous elephants in war belonged to Hannibal, the Carthaginian general. In 216 BCE he brought them from Spain to fight against Rome at the battle of Cannae in southern Italy.

WAR BEASTS
Elephants are not aggressive by nature but could be used to frighten troops who had never seen them before. A panicking elephant could trample its own soldiers. In India, handlers called mahouts carried a spike. If their elephant went out of control, they killed it.

◀ ELEPHANT POWER
The elephant has three natural weapons: its great weight, its huge tusks and its powerful trunk.

▲ THE HEAVY BRIGADE
Elephants were used on the front line of battle to frighten the enemy infantry and to block cavalry charges. Like modern tanks, they were protected from close range attack by special groups of foot soldiers.

▼ ARMOR
The Indians put armor on their elephants as well as fighting towers on their backs.

One of the earliest battles to use war elephants was fought at Arbela, now modern Irbil, in 331 BCE. The Persian leader Darius led an army, including 15 war elephants, against Alexander the Great of Macedonia. Alexander's troops were frightened of the elephants at first, but so well-disciplined that they did not run away but fought and won the battle.

War elephants had been used in India by the Hindus from around 400 BCE. They were as important as chariots on the battlefield. At the battle of Hydaspes in India in 327 BCE, Porus, the Rajah of Lahore, led elephants against Alexander the Great. This time, Alexander's horses were frightened by the elephants. However, his foot soldiers attacked the elephants with battleaxes. The animals panicked, and the Macedonians won.

The most famous war elephants belonged to Hannibal, the Carthaginian general. He fought against Rome in the Second Punic War (218–203 BCE). The elephants were used in several battles, but Hannibal was eventually beaten.

Elephants were first seen in England in 43 CE when the Romans used them to invade. War elephants were still in use in India during the 18th century. The elephants had iron plates fixed to their heads and were driven forward like four-legged battering rams to break down the gates of the town of Arcot in 1751. They panicked when they were fired at by muskets and stampeded.

▲ CAMEL ARMY
The camel has been used for transport in battle in the Middle East. It has lots of stamina and can move fast. Camels can also travel a long way without much food or water. Here, camel-mounted soldiers use lances and swords in a lively battle.

◀ OVER THE ALPS
Hannibal marched with his elephants across the Pyrenees and the Alps to attack Imperial Rome. When he set out from Saguntum in 218 BCE, he had 50,000 infantry, 9,000 cavalry and about 80 elephants. By the time he reached the Po valley in northern Italy six months later, only a few elephants were still alive. Hannibal had lost 30,000 infantry and 3,000 cavalry.

Key Dates

- 327 BCE Battle of Hydaspes. Alexander the Great meets Indian elephants.

- 275 BCE Battle of Benevenetum, Italy. Carthage uses elephants for the first time against Rome.

- 218 BCE Hannibal crosses the Alps.

- 202 BCE Battle of Zama. Hannibal defeated and his elephants taken.

- 190 BCE Battle of Magnesia. Syrian war elephants panic and confuse their own troops.

- CE 43 Roman Emperor Claudius uses elephants to invade Britain.

Horses in Battle

Horses MADE IT POSSIBLE for armies to move around quickly. They could pull wagons and siege weapons or carry loot and possessions. On the battlefield, they could be ridden by scouts or messengers taking news to and from the generals planning the battle. Large horses, working together as heavy cavalry, were unstoppable on the battlefield.

The first people to use the horse in war were the Assyrians around 800 BCE. They used them as cavalry, to pull chariots and for hunting. The Romans bred from European, Middle Eastern and African stock to produce racehorses, hunters, chargers and harness-horses.

The saddle with stirrups, which were probably invented in China, reached Europe in the 2nd century CE and transformed mounted operations forever. They made it easier to ride a horse. A Roman soldier on foot could cover about 5 miles (8 km) a day. When he was on a horse, he could travel twice as far as that.

The horse also made it possible for groups of people to move far away from their home lands. In the 13th century, the Mongols roamed from Central Asia as far as Vietnam, the Middle East and Europe.

There were two kinds of cavalry, the light and the heavy. The difference between them was based on the size of the horse. Most ancient armies had both light and heavy cavalry. About two-thirds of the Mongol riders

▲ PARTING SHOT
Horse archers from Parthia, an ancient country now part of Iran, used to pretend to retreat then turned and fired their arrows backwards to take the enemy by surprise.

◄ A LIGHT SKIRMISH
Persian light cavalry troops, carrying round shields and armed with lances and maces, fight a running battle.

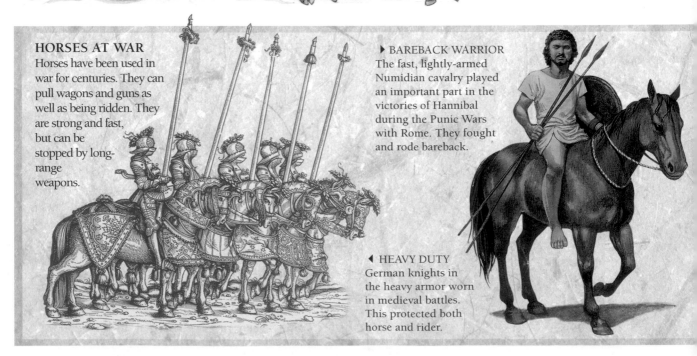

HORSES AT WAR
Horses have been used in war for centuries. They can pull wagons and guns as well as being ridden. They are strong and fast, but can be stopped by long-range weapons.

▶ BAREBACK WARRIOR
The fast, lightly-armed Numidian cavalry played an important part in the victories of Hannibal during the Punic Wars with Rome. They fought and rode bareback.

◄ HEAVY DUTY
German knights in the heavy armor worn in medieval battles. This protected both horse and rider.

▼ JOUSTING TOURNAMENT
Today, tournaments and battles are reenacted by "knights" on horseback.

▶ AT THE CHARGE
The horse wears a piece of head armor called a chauffron. Its spike is almost as much of a weapon as the rider's lance. Both are pointed towards the enemy when the horse charges.

were light cavalry. They had small, fast horses, wore protective helmets and carried bows and arrows. The heavy cavalry had big, strong horses, wore mail armor or heavy leather clothing and were armed with lances.

Armies in medieval Europe had only foot soldiers and knights on horseback. To carry a knight in full armor the horse had to be big and strong. The knights were a kind of heavy cavalry. By the 16th century, the armies of Europe had concentrated on heavy cavalry. The French called them gendarmerie and the Germans called them Schwarzreiter or "Black Riders." It was when they fought with Turkish armies in the 17th century that Europeans began to see how useful a light cavalry could be and to set up light brigades of their own. The Hungarian light cavalry, called hussars, wore Turkish-style uniforms.

The heavy cavalry wore helmets and breastplates, rode large horses and carried a pistol and heavy saber. The light cavalry had no armor and rode horses chosen for their speed. The riders carried two or even three pistols and a light sword.

The Tulughma

Heavy Cavalry   Light Cavalry

◀ MONGOLIAN WAR TACTICS
The Mongolian army used light and heavy cavalry and many different tactics. This one is the tulughma. The heavy brigade led the charge and broke up enemy lines. At the same time they protected the ranks of light cavalry behind them. When the enemy ranks were broken, the lighter horses ran through or round their own heavy ranks.

Key Dates

- 500 BCE Persians employ lancers and horse archers.

- 53 BCE Parthian horse archers defeat Romans at Carrhae (modern Iraq).

- CE 100s Stirrup introduced to Europe.

- 200–400 Horse archers and lancers used by Romans.

- 977–1030 Mahmud of Ghazni uses cavalry horse archers in north India.

- 1000–1200 Crusaders use Moslem mercenaries called Turcopoles.

- 1396–1457 French cavalry, gendarmes, in action.

- 1500–1600 German "Black Riders" in action in Europe.

Chariots and War Wagons

him was free to concentrate on fast and accurate firing at the enemy.

Not all chariots were two-man vehicles. If there was only one rider, he would tie the reins around his waist to keep his hands free so he could use his weapons. Some chariots, pulled by three or four horses, could carry several men, armed with a variety of weapons. Used all together, chariots could break up ranks of enemy infantry. Some later chariots had the protection of armor. They may also have had blades or scythes fitted to the hubs of their wheels to prevent enemy infantry or cavalry approaching too close. The drawback with chariots, like many wheeled vehicles, was that they could bog down in mud and it was hard for them to cross rough ground.

Between 1420 and 1434, the Hussites, a group of people from Bohemia (now the Czech

CHARIOTS WERE A CLEVER WAY to combine speed and action. Most of them were pulled by horses. The driver was called a charioteer. For the armies of ancient Egypt, Assyria, Persia, India and China, chariots were the weapon of surprise, racing in and out of battle. Most chariots held two people, the driver and the bowman. With the driver to handle the horse or horses, the archer riding beside

▲ ROMAN CHARIOT
The chariot was not used a great deal in war. It was a popular sight at the public Games held in Rome and other major cities of the Empire.

▶ EGYPTIAN TACTICS
An Egyptian courtier on a hunting trip fires his bow and arrows from a moving chariot. The same skills would be used in war.

▲ WARRIOR QUEEN
Boudicca, chieftain of the British tribe called the Iceni, used war chariots in her battles against invading Romans.

WHEELS OF WAR
Chariots were first used in the Bronze Age in the 15th century BCE in the Middle East. They could be pulled by two to four horses, but the larger number were harder to control. They could move easily on the flat deserts of Egypt and around the Euphrates, but they were not ideal transport in muddy, broken or rocky terrain. The war wagons used by the Hussites in Europe in the 15th century CE were almost like the first tanks. They were formed into circles like mobile forts. Soldiers fired cannons and muskets from the shelter of the wagons.

▲ LEONARDO'S TANKS
Leonardo da Vinci, the genius of the Renaissance, had many ideas that were ahead of his time. This sketch shows armored vehicles of various kinds. They look like early versions of modern tanks.

In 15th-century Europe, horses and carts were used to haul heavy cannons around the battlefield. This meant that the guns could be taken to positions where they could be most use. As artillery troops became more mobile they could do more harm to the enemy.

cavalry at bay. There were 350 wagons in a Wagenburg, linked together with chains and sometimes dug in. Within the circle of wagons were 700 cavalrymen and 7,000 infantry. Gaps closed with chains, posts and spikes could be opened to allow the Hussite cavalry out to attack. When the Hussites brought in cannon mounted on special wagons, the German cavalry refused to attack them any more because they were too dangerous.

Republic), fought with the Germans. The Hussites were followers of the religious reformer John Huss. Their army, commanded by Jan Zizka, used armored carts. The wagons were formed into a circle of wagons called a Wagenburg, or wagon castle. Behind the wagons, crossbow archers and musketeers kept the German

Some historians have suggested that the Hussite Wagenburg was the first tank in history as it combined fire power, protection and movement.

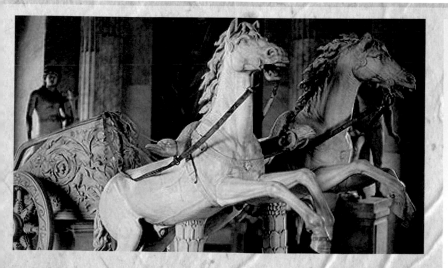

▲ CHARIOTS OF MARBLE
Many artists have made paintings and sculptures of chariots. This Roman sculpture of a chariot and a pair of frisky horses is in the Vatican Museum.

Key Dates

- 1400 BCE Chariots used by Egyptians.
- 331 BCE Persian chariots armed with scythes at Battle of Arbela.
- 327 BCE Indian chariots used at Battle of Hydaspes.
- 225 BCE Last use of chariots by Celts in Battle of Telamon, Italy.
- CE 60 Boudicca uses chariots against the Romans in Britain.
- 378 Romans use wagons to defeat Goths at Adrianople (modern Turkey).
- 1420–34 Fighting wagons used by Jan Zizka and the Hussites.

Cavalry Weapons

THE WEAPON USED BY A MOUNTED soldier reflected his skills as a rider. The Mongol cavalry riders of Genghis Khan could ride without reins, which meant they were able to use a bow while in the saddle. The lance or spear could be used in one hand. It was long enough for a rider to reach enemy foot soldiers. Cavalry normally rode straight at their enemy using the speed and impetus of the horse to add weight to the lance thrust. The cavalry lance became popular in medieval Europe and continued to be used in battle by horsemen in Poland and Hungary. Polish Lancers used it against the French during the Napoleonic Wars in 1800–1815. Medieval knights used the lance in battle, and practiced their skill in tournaments. The knight's horse also became a target, so craftsmen began to make armor for horses. Horse armor was called bard. At its simplest it was made up of the chauffron, a plate covering the front of the horse's skull, and the peytral, which covered the breast above the front legs. Full horse armor included the crupper and the flanchard. The crupper covered the horse's rump. The flanchard was an oblong plate fixed to the base of the saddle. It protected the horse's flanks and closed the gap between the crupper and peytral.

European cavalry troopers had been using straight swords from Roman times. When fighting in the Middle

▲ PERSIAN HORSEMAN
The light cavalry trooper of the Persian army carried a short spear. His horse was not protected by armor so was fast and nimble.

▲ SAMURAI BOWMAN
Japanese samurai warriors did not only use swords. Many were also masters of the longbow. A mounted archer on a trained horse had two advantages. He could move fast and he could fire his weapon from a distance, out of the range of his enemy's swords and lances.

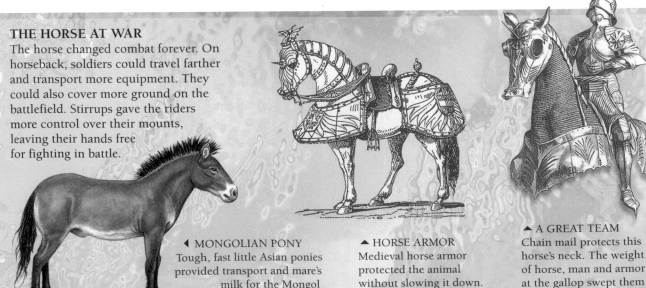

THE HORSE AT WAR
The horse changed combat forever. On horseback, soldiers could travel farther and transport more equipment. They could also cover more ground on the battlefield. Stirrups gave the riders more control over their mounts, leaving their hands free for fighting in battle.

◀ MONGOLIAN PONY
Tough, fast little Asian ponies provided transport and mare's milk for the Mongol warriors as they crossed Europe.

▲ HORSE ARMOR
Medieval horse armor protected the animal without slowing it down. The rider's legs covered its bare flanks in battle.

▲ A GREAT TEAM
Chain mail protects this horse's neck. The weight of horse, man and armor at the gallop swept them through the ranks of the enemy's foot soldiers.

▼ TOURNAMENT
When jousting for sport, knights used blunted lances so that they would not harm each other.

Chauffron

Blunted lance

Knight's insignia

East, European soldiers came across the curved sword, which was used as a pattern for the curved cavalry saber. This was ideal for the slashing backstroke.

The wheel lock pistol was developed in the 16th century. It was designed to be used with one hand so that the rider could shoot while keeping full control of his horse. Because of the noise, flashing and smoke, horses had to be trained to carry men through gunfire.

▶ GOING WEST
In 1190 the Mongol emperor Genghis Khan led his great army westward. It was divided into groups of 10,000 men called hordes. The hordes were named after different colors. Ogodai, Monkai, Kublai Khan and Tamerlane were later Mongol leaders who continued to expand deep into eastern Europe, reaching almost as far as Austria.

Western Christendom

Golden Horde

Byzantium

Blue Horde   White Horde

Kwarzim

Mongol Union   China

Gobi Desert

Sung

Moghul Empire

〜〜〜 Great Wall of China
← Conquests of Genghis Khan
← Conquests of Ogodai
← Conquests of Monkai and Kublai Khan
← Conquests of Tamerlane

0   Kilometers   3000
0   Miles   2000

N

Key Dates

- 400s BCE Persian mounted archers.

- 400 BCE Spartan cavalry armed with short javelins.

- 330s BCE Alexander the Great uses mounted lancers.

- 200s BCE Hannibal uses Numidian mounted lancers.

- 1200s Mongol hordes, mounted on horseback, invade Europe.

- 1300s–1500s Jousting lances in use.

- 1400s Heavy horse armor introduced.

- 1600s Sabers introduced as cavalry weapons.

Castles and Fortifications

THERE ARE NUMEROUS EXAMPLES of prehistoric and ancient fortifications throughout the world. The people who built them often used natural features such as hills, cliffs and crags or rivers, lakes and swamps to enhance their strength. Where these features were not present, people created them, making ditches, mounds and later walls and towers. Sometimes castle builders used earlier sites. For example, at Porchester in Hampshire in the 1120s, Henry I built a motte-and-bailey castle using the square fortifications of an earlier Roman Saxon fort.

The outlines of square Roman forts can be seen throughout Europe. These forts were called castra, which is where we get the word castle. Castra were built by legionary soldiers as a secure base at the end of a

▶ THE MEDIEVAL CASTLE
This typical castle has crennelated walls, which meant the defenders could shoot through the gaps.

Crenellation

Gatehouse

Drawbridge

Portcullis

◀ SCOTTISH CASTLE
Caerlavarock Castle, Scotland, is a classic moated castle. The pattern of stone bricks on the top of the round towers is known as machicolation. It is to protect soldiers inside the towers as they fight off an attack. The moat that surrounds the walls gives even more protection. The castle was hard to storm.

CASTLES FROM MUD TO STONE

The earliest fortifications were made from earth. Mud bricks and stone were used in the Middle East. The Romans were the first to build fortifications in Europe. In Britain after the Norman Conquest of 1066, the Normans built a large number of castles. These became the foundations for many of the great medieval castles. Crusader knights brought back many castle-building techniques from the Middle East.

▶ STONE CASTLES
Later castles were built of stone. The central keep is surrounded by curtain walls to defend it from attack.

▲ MOTTE-AND-BAILEY
These simple wooden forts were built by the Normans. The motte, on the raised mound, was where the family and servants lived. The bailey was the walled yard for animals and food stores.

◀ NORMAN TOWER
To replace the wooden forts, Normans built square stone keeps. The most famous example is the White Tower of the Tower of London.

Keep

Moat

Curtain wall

march in hostile territory. Sometimes these temporary bases became more permanent. They were called Castra Stativa. Rations, stores and baggage could be dumped there while lightly-armed legionaries patrolled enemy territory.

Norman motte-and-bailey castles in England were built as bases for the occupying power after the defeat of King Harold at Hastings in 1066. The medieval castle was a base for a lord or baron. It was defended by a large garrison of soldiers. Towns grew up around the castles and, if the community was wealthy, they would build strong walls around the outside. Knights and nobles who had fought in the crusades against the Saracens brought back many new ideas about castle design. The curtain wall surrounding the castle was a Saracen idea. For the baron in his castle or the citizens of a town, the time and resources expended improving the defenses were like an insurance policy against bad times.

◀ WELSH CASTLES
In the 13th century, King Edward I of England built a large number of castles in Wales. This was to strengthen his grip on the country. The Welsh people did not care for English rule. Craftsmen were brought from all over England to help in the building work. Edward's wife and queen, Eleanor, gave birth to their first son, the future Edward II, at Caernarfon Castle. He became the Prince of Wales, the first English man to hold the title.

Key Dates

- 2500 BCE Ur of the Chaldees, first fortified city, built (in modern Iraq).

- 701 BCE Jerusalem fortified.

- 560 BCE Athens fortified.

- 1058–1689 Edinburgh Castle.

- 1066–1399 Tower of London.

- 1181–89 Dover Castle.

- 1196–98 Chateau-Gaillard built by Richard I in France.

- 1200s Krak des Chevaliers, a Crusader castle, built in Syria.

- 1538–1540s Henry VIII builds forts along England's south coast.

Towers, Keeps and Gates

To DEFEND THEIR CASTLES, people built tall towers and keeps. Standing at the top, they could see enemy ships or army columns a long way off. This gave the people in the castle time to prepare for attack. When the enemy arrived at the castle walls, the lookouts on the tower could see down into their camps or siege weapons and fire missiles at them. Towers can be square or round, but always have very thick walls.

Towers are safe places to hide when an enemy attacks. In the 9th and 10th centuries, Vikings raided England and Ireland. To defend themselves, Irish people built high towers in villages or near monasteries. These stone-built towers had no outer defenses. They had arrow slits or embrasures and a simple door built high up the wall that could only be reached using a ladder.

After the Norman Conquest of England, Norman barons built many castles. They were mostly of the motte-and-bailey kind. A curtain wall stood around the bailey. Towers were built at the corners of the wall and at intervals along the sides. Soldiers could use the towers as safe bases. The towers had a thicker belt of stone at the base. This was called a batter. It was meant to strengthen the towers against battering rams and make it difficult to mine through the walls.

The gate was the weakest part of the castle. It was protected by a gatehouse and a portcullis. Some

◀ IRISH DEFENSES
The high towers of Ireland were built as refuges from invading Vikings. They were not intended to hold out against a long siege but were good look-outs and safe places to hide.

▶ BAMBURGH CASTLE
Bamburgh Castle Keep, in Northumberland, England, dates from 1200. The keep was the strongest part of a castle.

THE KEY TO THE CASTLE
The gate was the most vulnerable part of a castle because it was the point of entrance. When it was open, attackers could force their way in, and the castle could be captured very quickly. It was very important that the opening could be closed quickly. An iron gate called a portcullis could be dropped into place in seconds. The drawbridge only needed to be lifted a short way to prevent the enemy crossing the moat.

▶ DRAWBRIDGE
The drawbridge was made from very thick wood. It could be raised very quickly. It was operated by a system of weights which worked in the same way as a see-saw.

◀ PORTCULLIS
The portcullis was operated by a winch. The guards could release it quickly, and let it crash down under its own weight. Spikes on the bottom of the portcullis could trap attackers caught underneath it.

gatehouses had two portcullises. Attackers could be lured through the open gate only to find their way barred by an inner portcullis or gate hidden around a corner. Once the attackers were inside, the defenders would lower the outer portcullis and trap them. The passage between the gates became a stone tunnel. In the roof of the tunnel were slots known as "murder holes." Defenders could shoot arrows, drop rocks or pour boiling oil or water through the holes on to their trapped enemies.

Spiral staircases could be defended by one swordsman

Guard on lookout duty

The nobleman's bedroom

Thick walls

The dining hall

▶ THE KEEP
At the center of the castle was the keep. It was where the family lived and where food and weapons were stored. If the enemy broke through the curtain walls, the keep was the last resort. To survive a siege, keeps had their own well to provide a reliable supply of water.

Well for fresh water

Storeroom for supplies

Walls

Castle walls were built to a set pattern. Surrounding the castle was a curtain wall. This could be 16 to 26 feet (5 to 8 m) thick and wide enough for people to walk along. On top of the wall was the parapet. The parapet was a wall about 1.6 feet (.5 m) thick. In some castles they were built only at the top of the outer face of the wall. Others had them on both sides. They were about 6.6 feet (2 m) high, so that they completely concealed and protected any soldier standing guard on the curtain wall.

Along the parapets were regular gaps which were low and wide enough for an archer to shoot at enemies. The gaps were called crenellations. The sections of raised wall between the gaps, which protected the archer, were called merlons.

At intervals in the wall and in towers of the castle, the builders cut narrow windows from which archers

▲ KEEPING THE NIGHT WATCH
Castles were defended day and night. Norman soldiers on the parapet check on the sentries manning the gatehouse and curtain wall defenses below.

could fire. These were called embrasures. When soldiers began to use cannons, the embrasures were made larger to fit the muzzles of the guns. Circular holes were cut at the base of arrow slits so that both the artillery men and the archers could fire from the same embrasure. This embrasure was known as a "cross-and-orb." Larger embrasures were covered by hinged shutters when they were not being used. From the outside, an embrasure looked like a narrow slit. On the inside, it opened up so that an archer could lean to one side and shoot at targets to the left or right. A variation on this design was the balistraria, a cross-shaped slit for crossbows.

If an enemy force reached the base of a wall, the defenders had to lean out to attack them. This would leave them open to attack by enemy archers. The castle builders invented machicolation, which was made to

SLITS AND EMBRASURES
The walls and crenellations of castles were pierced with holes called embrasures. These were made so that the soldiers could fire arrows or crossbow bolts at their enemy below. Later, castle walls were pierced with loopholes for cannon and muskets. The hole was shaped to fit the kind of weapon being fired through it. On the inside face of the wall, the sides of the embrasure were angled so that an archer or musketeer could shoot at targets to one side.

▼ ARCHER'S SLIT
The earliest kind of slit was made to fit arrows. Arrow slits also let light and air in to the inside of the castle and through the curtain walls.

▲ CROSSBOW EMBRASURE
This design was used by crossbow archers. It allowed them to aim at targets to the left or right of them, or even to track a moving target before firing their bolts.

▼ LOOPHOLE
When cannons began to be used, arrow holes were changed to fit them. A round hole was cut at the base of a narrow slit.

◀ CARCASSONNE
This walled city in southern France looks much the same today as it did in medieval times. With such strong defenses, the only way an enemy could capture the city would be to starve the citizens.

▲ WINDSOR CASTLE
The towers on each side of the gatehouse at Windsor have machicolations at the top.

protect the defenders. This was a battlement wall built out on stone supports. It had embrasures that faced downward so that defenders could drop rocks and stones on their attackers.

Henry VIII made many changes in the design of fortresses. To fight off the threat of French invasion in the mid-16th century, he built a number of forts along the south coast of England. Their walls were not high, but low and massive. This was to provide a wide platform for cannons and large guns to stand on. As the power and range of cannons got better, the walls of fortifications became wider and lower.

◀ WALLS WITHIN WALLS
The Roman general Scipio, also known as Africanus, built a wall with seven forts around the Spanish city of Numantia. He then besieged the city for eight months in 133 BCE. Its 4,000 citizens finally gave in after Scipio had blocked off the river access.

▶ CITY WALLS
In ancient times cities were often under threat of attack and invasion. It was common to build fortified walls around the city for protection. This imposing wall surrounds the Moroccan city of Essaouira.

Key Dates

- 1451 BCE Walls of Jericho stormed.
- 598 BCE Nebuchadnezzar destroys the walls of Jerusalem.
- 493 BCE Piraeus, the port of Athens, made secure with fortifications.
- 478 BCE Athenian city walls restored.
- 457 BCE Athenian long wall built.
- 393 BCE Conon rebuilds long walls at Athens following their destruction by the Persians.
- CE 93–211 Walls of Perge (southern Turkey) built by Septimus Severus.
- 447 Ramparts of Constantinople rebuilt after earthquake.

Defending Borders

MOST FORTIFICATIONS in ancient history have normally protected families and their retainers in castles, or citizens behind curtain walls with fortified gates. When the movement of large numbers of people threatens a civilization, bigger walls have to be built. The Great Wall of China and Hadrian's Wall in England are two very famous examples of land barriers made to defend whole territories.

▲ THE GREAT WALL
Large enough to be seen from space, this famous earthwork in China took centuries to build.

The Great Wall of China was built over four distinct periods. The building of earthworks in 476–221 BCE was followed by the Great Wall of Qin Shi Huangdi (221–206 BCE). The Great Wall of Wu Di (140–86 BCE) and other emperors was finally finished as the Great Wall of the Mings (1368–1644 CE). The Great Wall of China was originally built to delay Mongol attacks along the north frontier long enough for the main force of the Chinese army to get to the threatened area and defeat the enemy.

The Roman Emperor Hadrian toured northern Britain in 122 CE and ordered the construction of a physical barrier against the lawless tribes in Caledonia (modern Scotland). At first, the barrier was made from timber and turf. In its final form, Hadrian's Wall was just a stone wall. It ran from Wallsend on the east coast

▶ HADRIAN'S WALL
Named after the Roman Emperor Hadrian, the wall was originally a wooden palisade with a bank and ditch. It was later rebuilt as a stone-faced wall 16 feet (5 m) high and 8 feet (2.5 m) thick. Small emplacements called mile castles were placed at every mile along the wall.

Roman legionary

THE WORLD'S EDGE
The Romans and the Chinese had huge empires to guard. Just beyond their borders were people ready to invade. To mark and defend their borders, they built long walls or earthworks. A system of signaling allowed sentries to alert the garrisons if raiders tried to cross the wall. Then soldiers could quickly get to the site to drive them off.

◀ LEGIONARY FROM AFRICA
Roman soldiers were recruited from all parts of the enormous empire. They were often sent on duty far away from their home country. This was to make sure they did not desert.

▲ WALLS AROUND WALLS
The Romans used walls and ramparts as weapons in their siege tactics, closing off a city or fort from any outside assistance or supplies and starving it into surrender. This is the siege of Massilia laid by Julius Caesar in 49 BCE. Massilia is modern-day Marseilles.

◀ MILE CASTLES
Protected from the Picts (the painted people) from the north by Hadrian's Wall, small towns grew up around the mile castles along the Wall. There were shops and markets, taverns and baths. Many of the Roman legionaries who manned the Wall married and settled down in the towns.

to Bowness in the west, a distance of approximately 73 miles (118 km). The wall used natural features such as crags to give it extra height. It varied from 7.5 to 9.8 feet (2.3 to 3 m) in width and was 15 feet (4.5 m) high with a crenellated parapet 5 feet (1.5 m) above that. There were mile castles along the wall at regular intervals of one Roman mile (1480 m) and two guard turrets between them. The mile castle was in a kind of gateway with a garrison of about 16 soldiers. The turrets may have been shelters for soldiers on guard or signal stations. Ten forts were built to house the garrison for the wall.

Hadrian's Wall was an effective military obstacle, and, like similar Roman barriers, it marked the limits of the Roman Empire. Beyond it were barbarians.

▶ JERUSALEM
The walls of the Holy City have been stormed and fought over ever since biblical times. Jerusalem is a city divided into the Jewish western area and the Arab territory in the east. The last battle took place in 1967 during the Six Day War between the Arabs and the Israelis.

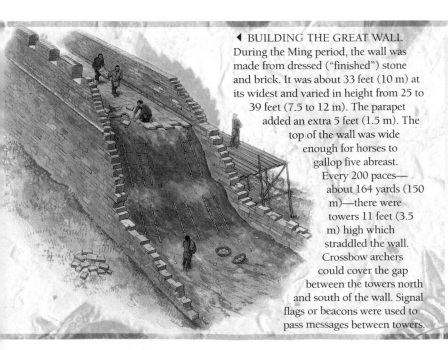

◀ BUILDING THE GREAT WALL
During the Ming period, the wall was made from dressed ("finished") stone and brick. It was about 33 feet (10 m) at its widest and varied in height from 25 to 39 feet (7.5 to 12 m). The parapet added an extra 5 feet (1.5 m). The top of the wall was wide enough for horses to gallop five abreast. Every 200 paces—about 164 yards (150 m)—there were towers 11 feet (3.5 m) high which straddled the wall. Crossbow archers could cover the gap between the towers north and south of the wall. Signal flags or beacons were used to pass messages between towers.

Key Dates

- 476–221 BCE Various earth walls built in northern Chinese provinces.

- 221–206 BCE Emperor Qin Shi Huangdi orders earth walls to be joined together to make the first Great Wall of China.

- CE 100 Romans build walls (called limes germanica) across Germany and Romania.

- CE 122 Emperor Hadrian orders wall to be built at northern edge of Roman Empire.

- 700s King Offa of Mercia, England, builds a dike to separate England from Wales.

Under Siege

A SIEGE IS WHAT happens when an enemy army surrounds a castle or a city planning to capture it. They can attack, or they can wait until the people inside get too hungry and surrender. A strong, well-stocked castle or fortified town could easily withstand a siege if their besiegers ran out of food. The defenders of a castle or even the wall around a town were higher up than the besiegers so they could see what the enemy was doing. They were also protected by a wooden palisade or a stone wall. From behind these walls, sniper archers could pick off the attackers as they came to the foot of the wall.

If the attackers reached the wall, they tried to make a hole in it so that they could get into the castle or city. Another way to get in was to climb the wall using ladders and grapnel hooks. This was dangerous, because the defenders waited until an attacker was half way up the ladder then pushed it away from the wall.

To attack the enemy camp the soldiers of the castle could use many of the weapons that the besiegers had been using. Each side lobbed rocks or cannon balls at one another. If a battering ram was used, the defenders might try to set fire to it.

▲ OUT OF RANGE
Building a castle on a hill site with a moat and a narrow, easily guarded entry road makes it very hard for an enemy to capture it.

Another way to disarm it was to use huge tongs hanging from a crane to grab the ram and pull it up inside the castle or curtain walls.

Castles often had secret passages leading to a hidden exit called a "sally port." This could be farther down a river or along the coast, and from here the defenders might make their escape if the siege became too severe. Sally ports were also very strong doors from which the defenders could launch quick raids on their attackers. The plan was to destroy the enemy's siege weapons, generally by setting them alight. The defenders would also capture prisoners and steal food stocks.

▶ HOT RECEPTION
As storming ladders are raised against a castle, defenders fight back by pouring boiling water or oil on the shed protecting a battering ram crew.

HOLDING OUT
Siege was not always easy for the besiegers. If the castle was well defended and the people inside had lots of water and food supplies, they could sit out any number of attacks. If the siege went on for a long time, the besiegers could run out of food themselves, or die from disease and be forced to stop the siege.

◀ SIEGE SEESAW
The tenelon was a crane or seesaw with a basket on one arm. Troops inside the basket could be hoisted over the walls.

▲ WHO'S WINNING?
Every kind of siege weapon is used against the defenders in this castle keep. They are fighting back but seem to be outnumbered and may be running out of food. One of the soldiers is lowering a basket and water pot for supplies.

◀ A CASTLE FALLS
Battering rams, scaling ladders and towers can all be seen in action in this medieval siege. It is the end of the siege. The walls have been finally breached after heavy bombardment, and the besiegers are within the walls.

◀ ROMAN SIEGE
The Roman army were very successful at sieges. They invented many techniques and siege engines. In this scene, the besiegers are attacking on three points. A ram batters at the tower. Soldiers advance under cover of their shields locked into the testudo, or tortoise, formation. Some have reached the wall and are scaling it. A tenelon hoists men on to the far tower. The defenders crowd the battlements, but they only have rocks to throw at the enemy.

Key Dates

- 415–413 BCE Siege of Syracuse. Athenians fail to take city.

- CE 70 Siege of Jerusalem, part of the Jewish Wars of the Roman Empire.

- 1189–91 Siege of Acre (Israel), part of the Third Crusade.

- 1487 Siege of Malaga.

- 1544 Siege of Boulogne.

- 1565 Siege of Malta, part of the wars of Islam. Turkish army try to capture Malta from Christian forces. They fail.

- 1688-89 Siege of Londonderry.

Siege Attack

THE ROMANS HAD A VERY SUCCESSFUL method of siege attack. First, they would take a good look at the target fort or city to see if a siege would be practical. They would then surround their objective with an outer belt of defenses so that it could not be relieved by friendly forces and set about systematically destroying it. Several specialist weapons were needed to do this. The most important was the siege tower.

Historic pictures of siege towers often show something that looks like a mobile multi-story building. The height varied. The three iron-clad towers used by the Romans in the Siege of Jerusalem in 70 CE were 33 feet (10 m) high with catapults on top. The towers were fitted with drawbridges that were lowered to span the gap to the castle wall. The military engineers Gaston de Bearn and William de Ricou, employed by the Crusaders in 1099 in another siege of Jerusalem, designed

two towers of about the same height as the ones the Romans used.

The earliest descriptions we have of siege weapons come from around 400 to 200 BCE. Among them were those developed by the engineer Diades, who worked with Alexander the Great. Diades developed two unusual siege weapons, which do not seem to have been copied by future generations. The first one was a mural hook, also known as a crow. It was slung from a wooden gantry like a ram, but it had a huge double clawed hook. This was used to pull down the

▶ ANCIENT ATTACKERS
Babylonian siege machines batter down the walls of an enemy fortress while archers fire on the walls.

Siege tower

Animal skin covering

Battering ram

▲ SIEGE GRIFFIN
A fantasy siege engine designed to be winched towards the enemy as it fires the cannon from its mouth. The ramp in the chest would be lowered for the assault.

SIEGE TOWERS
In order to reach the top of the walls and take on the defenders, soldiers had to be at the same height and within range. Mobile siege towers could be pushed forward until the soldiers inside them could fire at the enemy and eventually cross simple drawbridges on to the walls.

Mantlet

◀ ALEXANDER
Alexander the Great was a fine general. He laid many sieges. The best known was the Siege of Tyre, a fortified town. It lasted for seven months.

▲ MOBILE SHIELD
The mantlet was either a row of fixed hurdles, or in this example, a mobile shield that could be wheeled close to the enemy wall to give cover to archers.

battlements along the top of a city or fortress wall. The second was the telenon, a kind of crane. A large box or basket hung from it. Soldiers got into the basket and were swung on to the enemy's walls to attack.

Smaller items were also used. Scaling ladders were lightweight ladders, sometimes with hooks at the top. The besiegers used these to assault the walls. The soldiers would run forward, fix the ladders in position and scramble up them.

Grapnels or grappling hooks were hooks attached to a length of rope. Soldiers would throw the grapnel so that it hooked over the parapet of the wall and then climb up the rope.

While the soldiers were climbing the walls, archers would keep shooting from behind their mantlets to keep the enemy occupied. Otherwise the defenders would just cut the ropes or push away the ladders.

Another way to get inside was by using a trick. In the Trojan War between the Greeks and the Trojans, the Greeks pretended to give up. They gave the city of Troy a large wooden horse as a parting gift. The Trojans took it inside the city, not realizing that there were Greek

soldiers hiding inside the horse. Once inside the city walls, the Greeks jumped out and, after some fighting, they took the city and won the war.

▼ GOING IN
The drawbridge on an Assyrian siege tower crashes onto the enemy wall as the assault party storms in.

◀ ENGINEERS AT WAR
The Romans were masters of the planning and building work as well as the tactics of a siege. The siege of a large city was like a major engineering operation. Large numbers of timber structures had to be made very quickly and put into position. Sieges could go on for many years, so any building had to be quite sturdy.

Key Dates

- 612 BCE Nineveh (modern Iraq), capital of the Assyrian Empire, besieged and destroyed.

- 1346-47 Siege of Calais. Town officials prepare to die following surrender.

- 1429 Siege of Orleans relieved by Joan of Arc.

- 1453 Siege of Constantinople. Turks take the city ending the Holy Roman Empire.

- 1871 Siege of Paris. Citizens driven to eat zoo animals.

Bombardment

▲ GETTING YOUR OWN BACK
In this medieval picture, trebuchets are used to lob the severed heads of prisoners over the walls of a castle.

BEFORE SOLDIERS had cannons, bombardment weapons were built based on natural forces.

Classical and medieval siege weapons worked on one of three principles: spring tension, torsion or counterweight. Spring tension weapons were like giant crossbows. They used springy wood that bent easily, such as ash or yew.

Torsion means twisting. Torsion weapons were powered by twisted rope. The tighter it was wound up, the more power there was when it was released. This method could be used to fire stones or javelins. The Romans of the 3rd century CE nicknamed one of their torsion weapons onager, meaning "wild donkey." This was because of the violent kick of the machine's arm when the rope was released. They used a rope made from human hair for this weapon as it was very elastic.

The ballista was a little like a crossbow. The tension was produced by bending two lengths of wood held in coiled cord or braided hair.

The counterweight weapon or trebuchet reached Europe from China around 500 CE. It was like a giant seesaw with a heavy weight at one end and a sling at the other. A stone or other missile was placed in the sling, which was tied down so the heavy weight was in the air. When it was released, the weighted end would drop and lob the stone.

Stones were not the only thing that the trebuchet threw. Burning materials were hurled over the walls to try to start fires. Corpses of humans and animals were also thrown. This was to spread infection and to bring down the spirits of the defenders.

Looking at these weapons today, they seem crude and simple. However, in medieval Europe, with its poor roads and simple carpentry tools, building a weapon such as a trebuchet or a catapult and bringing it into action was a very impressive feat.

▶ WILD DONKEY
The onager or wild donkey was developed about the 3rd century CE. It earned its name from the violent kick from the throwing arm when the ratchet was released.

Throwing arm   Release lever
Hair rope
Sling

ARCHIMEDES

▲ ARCHIMEDES
A Sicilian scientist, Archimedes designed weapons for the defenders of Syracuse during the siege of 213–212 BCE. His engines were very effective against the Roman fleet.

GUIDED MISSILES
Before gunpowder, muscle power was used to throw missiles at the enemy. Soldiers had to be very strong to stretch or twist the ropes and springs or lift the heavy counterweights that gave catapults and trebuchets their power.

▶ GREEK FIRE
Siege machines could be adapted to throw "Greek fire," a mixture of chemicals, over the walls to burn the enemy.

◀ MASS ATTACK
This machine was designed to fire a barrage of arrows or javelins at one time. It was probably not very accurate.

◀ BALLISTA
The Romans developed the ballista, a weapon to launch missiles at the enemy. It worked rather like a crossbow and could be adapted to suit various kinds of ammunition. A light field ballista such as this could fire stones or javelins.

▼ CATAPULT

Protected by a mantlet, three soldiers tighten the tension on a catapult while a fourth prepares a stone for launching. The largest catapults could fire a 50 pound (22.6 kg) stone as far as 399 yards (365 m).

▶ ROMAN INVASION

In 43 CE, the Romans invaded Britain in the south. They got as far north as the Plautian frontier, named after the Roman leader Plautus. Maiden Castle in Dorset was the site of a battle between the Britons and the Romans. At this battle, catapults and ballista were used by the Roman army. There had been a fort of some kind on this site since the Stone Age, but by the time the Romans came, it was well fortified by ramps, walls and dikes.

Key Dates

- 400–200 BCE Catapult introduced into Rome from Syria.

- 211 BCE Mounted crossbow, possibly designed by Archimedes, in use to defend Syracuse.

- CE 100 Greeks build a catapult with an iron frame.

- 101–107 Ballista used by Romans in the Dacian wars (central Europe).

- 300 Onager in use with Romans. It was still used in medieval times.

- 1250s Trebuchet in extensive use.

- 1000–1400 Spring engines used in medieval Europe.

Ramps, Rams and Mining

So that they could bring their weapons in closer to the enemy, besieging troops built ramps outside the walls of the city or castle. Ramps or causeways were needed to cross ditches or moats filled with water. Ideally more than one ramp would be built so that the enemy would not know where the main assault was going to fall. The Romans pioneered the technique of building a ramp, known as an agger, from hurdles— packed earth and stone.

Once the besieging forces had filled in the moat and built a ramp up to the enemy's walls, the battering ram was wheeled into position. The battering ram was one of the oldest siege weapons. It was made from a heavy tree trunk hung on chains from a timber frame. The whole thing was covered by a wooden shelter called a penthouse. The roof and walls of the penthouse were often covered with animal hides that were kept wet as a protection against fire.

The battering ram could have a metal knob, sometimes in the shape of a ram's head, which was mounted at the front end of the tree trunk. By swinging the ram and driving it against the wall, the soldiers operating it would, with time and effort, make a hole. Mining was another way to break through a city or

Wooden piles

Construction of ramp

Castle walls

Enemy siege tower

Piles collapsing

Tunnel

▲ ROMAN RAMP
The agger or ramp is protected by flanking towers. Soldiers work on the ramp under long protective sheds.

▶ UNDERMINING
Defenders could destroy a ramp by digging a tunnel under its wooden piles and setting fire to them to make the ramp collapse.

BATTERING TO VICTORY

The battering ram was the heavyweight siege weapon used to smash holes in the walls of a castle or town. There were many different designs. It was an accepted rule in Roman siege tactics that once the ram had been brought into action, the defenders within the fort or town could expect no mercy when the walls finally came down. So, a ram was a frightening weapon in more ways than one.

◀ DEMONSTRATION
This picture shows how an 11th-century ram worked. In a real battle, the ramming crew would be protected from fire and missiles by a penthouse.

▲ GREEK BATTERING RAM
This wheeled tower is a two-in-one weapon. The ram batters the wall whilst the arm above it pulls down the castle battlements.

▶ RAM TOWER
Rams could be carried on the shoulders or mounted on wheels. This ram tower was pushed forward on wheels or rollers until it was within range of the castle wall. The gantry structure allowed the crew to develop a good, powerful swing with the ram.

◀ HOOKING A RAM
A hook mounted on a crane grabbed the siege weapon, which could be lifted and dropped until it broke up.

castle wall. First, the attackers would build an easy-to-move shelter and put it against the wall. Protected under the shelter, the soldiers could begin to knock down the wall. They supported it with wooden beams so that it did not fall down too soon. When enough of the wall had been weakened in this way, a fire would be lit under the beams. When the beams had been weakened by the fire, the wall collapsed, and the besieging forces could then storm across the gap that had been created. The soldiers inside the castle could dig their own mine beneath the attackers' mine shaft. They could try to make the enemy's mine collapse, or fight underground.

▶ SYRACUSE
The map shows the Siege of Syracuse in 415 BCE by the Athenians. They built the square fort at Labdalum and a circular fort with surrounding siege walls. But Syracuse held out and inflicted Athens' greatest defeat. The Athenians lost nearly 200 ships and 40-50,000 soldiers.

Fort
Wall
Fleet
Athenians
Marsh

Euryalus
Labdalum
Epipolae Plateau
The Circle
Syracuse
R. Onopus
Great Harbour
Plemmyrium

N

0 Kilometers 3
0 Miles 2

Key Dates

- 429–427 BCE Plataea, in Greece, besieged using ramps and defeated by Spartans.

- 415–413 BCE Siege of Syracuse (Sicily). Archimedes, born in Syracuse, designs some of the defense machinery.

- 52 BCE Siege of Alesia in Gaul. Vercingetorix the Gaulish leader finally surrenders to Romans.

- CE 72 Siege of Masada, Jerusalem. Romans build ramps to get over the huge walls of the fortress. Many defenders kill themselves rather than be captured.

Gunpowder Arrives

▲ POWDER RECIPE
The formula for gunpowder—one part sulphur, six parts saltpeter and two parts charcoal—first written down by the Englishman Roger Bacon around 1242.

SOLID GUNPOWDER turns quickly into gas when burned. If it is loose, gunpowder produces a flash, a cloud of white smoke and not much noise. If it is enclosed, the noise and the explosive force increases. This produces energy that can be used to push a solid object along a tube, or to blow up a building. The first use of gunpowder

in battle in Europe was by the British at the Battle of Crécy (1346). King Edward is said to have had three to five guns which were called roundelades or pots de fer because of their bottle or pot shape. Early weapons fired stones or arrows similar to crossbow bolts.

Cannon design did not change much over three hundred years. Gunpowder was poured into the open end or muzzle, and then packed down with a rammer. The packed gunpowder was secured in place with wadding, which was rammed home. A cannon ball was then loaded. Loose gunpowder was poured down the touch hole, a small hole at the closed end of the cannon. It was lit using a slow match, a length of rope soaked in saltpeter, which would burn slowly. The explosion that followed pushed the cannon ball out of the gun muzzle. It could reach ranges of between 219 yards (200 m) and 766 yards (700 m) depending on

▶ WHEELED CANNON
Protected by a penthouse this cannon sits on a simple frame that allows the crew to move it around the castle to fire stones at the enemy battlements. The cannon is held in place with guy lines and pegs which absorb the recoil when it fires and ensure it is correctly aligned.

Penthouse

Cannon

Wooden frame

EXPLOSIVES
Gunpowder was first used in Europe for weapons in the 14th century. It had been used in China since the 11th century to fuel battlefield rockets. It was more powerful than ropes, counterweights or springs, but gave off great clouds of smoke.

Double cannon

◀ DOUBLE SHOT
These cannons are on a static mount and would be fired in quick succession against a wall or gate—almost like a double-barreled weapon.

▶ HAND MORTAR
A 16th-century short-barreled weapon used for lobbing shot into enemy ranks.

Hand mortar

▲ HAND CANNON
The hand cannon was first used in 1364 and was the first step toward hand guns as we know them today. The gunner had to support his heavy firearm with a forked pike to keep it steady.

▶ SNAKE GUN
This drawing by the artist Dürer shows a cannon called a serpentine as it was thought to look like a snake or serpent. Many early cast cannons were shaped to look like serpents.

Serpentine

the size of the cannon and the ball. By the 1860s, ranges for a 12 pound (5.5 kg) cannon ball fired using a 2 pound (1.1 kg) charge had increased to 1,620 yards (1,500 m).

The ninth Siege of Constantinople by the Turks from April to May 1453 is the first example of the power of cannons. Constantinople was then the capital of the Eastern Roman Empire. It was ruled by Constantine XI. The Turkish leader was Sultan Muhammed II. A

◀ ENGLISH GUNS
One gunner raises the mantlet as the other prepares to light the touch hole to fire the stone ball.

▲ CANNONS WITH COVER
Early cannons were built in a similar way to beer barrels. Lengthways cast iron strips were bound with iron hoops and mounted in a static wooden carriage.

Hungarian engineer called Urban made a very long bronze cannon for the Turks. It measured 26 feet (8 m) and was capable of throwing a 1,455 pound (660 kg) stone one mile (1.6 km). Loading and firing took some time, so the weapon could only fire seven times a day. After 12 days of heavy bombardment, the Turks had broken through the walls of the city. Constantinople fell on May 29, 1453.

Gunpowder

Fuse

▼ USING THE PETARD
The petard was attached with its muzzle pressed up against the wooden gate, and then the fuse was lit. It was a dangerous thing to do, particularly if the fuse was too short or burned too fast.

Wooden Gate

Petard

▲ PETARD
The petard was an explosive device designed especially to blast wooden gates. It was used by army engineers of the 15th and 16th centuries. It looked rather like a cut down cannon. It was about 11.8 inches (30 cm) long, 9.8 inches (25 cm) wide, weighed about 60 pounds (27 kg) and had a touch hole and open muzzle.

Key Dates

- 1242 Roger Bacon writes down the formula for gunpowder.

- 1324 Cannons believed to have been used at siege of Metz, in France.

- 1342 Reports of cannons at siege of Algeciras, Spain.

- 1346 Confirmed use of cannons at the battle of Crécy, France.

- 1450–1850 Most cannons were cast in bronze, iron or brass.

- 1500 Metal shot had replaced stone.

- 1571 At the battle of Lepanto, Greece, heavily gunned galleys were used.

War at Sea

▲ OAR POWER
There were many kinds of warship design. This is a Greek galley with a single bank of oars.

THE MEDITERRANEAN Sea was central to the ancient world. Its name means "in the middle of the earth." Many countries depended on it for food and trade. Whoever controlled the sea, therefore, had power over all the countries that surrounded it. The Mediterranean has hardly any tides. Ships were not dependent on the tide coming in to launch and could not become stranded when the tide went out. The sea became part of the battlefield. Fighting methods and weapons were much the same as they were on land. The key to sea fighting was transport. Fast boats with a reliable power source usually won the battle. The Greeks, Romans, Persians and Carthaginians all developed warships that could deliver troops quickly to the scene of the battle. As each would try to stop the other, they adapted land weapons for use at sea, such as grappling hooks, siege towers and catapults.

A good general used sea power to help his land battles. The tactics developed by the ancient sea captains still work today. The Athenian plan for the Battle of Salamis was so successful that it is taught in

▼ OARS AT WORK
There were three layers of galley slaves in a trireme. To be effective they had to be able to row in time, so they probably used a drum to keep the time. Clearly the best position was on the top row.

SEA POWER
Most warships relied on banks of galley slaves to row them into action. Some ships had sails that could be used when the wind was favorable.

◄ XERXES
This Persian king came to power in 486 BCE and launched a massive land and sea assault on Athens and her allies in 480 BCE but he was defeated.

▶ THE BATTLE OF SALAMIS
This classic sea battle was fought in 480 BCE between the Athenians led by Themistocles and the Persians under Xerxes.

N

◢◢◢ Greeks
◢◢◢ Persians

Bay of Eleusis

Xerxes command post

City of Salamis

Salamis Island

Megarian Channel

| 0 | Kilometers | 6 |
| 0 | Miles | 4 |

miltary school. The sea battle at Lepanto in 1571 was fought between Austria and the Turks; it was the last time galleys were used in war. Austria captured 130 Turkish galleys and destroyed 80 more. The battle ended Turkish control of the Mediterranean.

Different kinds of ships and skills were needed to deal with larger seas, more extreme weather and tides. Countries with coastlines on the Atlantic or Pacific built boats that could land in shallow water if the tide was out. The Vikings who sailed the Atlantic owed their success to their long, flat-bottomed boats, which could land almost anywhere.

Boats were used to deliver troops to a land battle or invasion. Vikings, Saxons, Danes and Normans invaded Great Britain by sea between 800 and 1066. During the Crusades in the Middle East, knights were brought from Europe by sea. Ships were also used to help in the sieges of coastal cities.

◀ TACTICS
The Persian fleet of 1,000 ships had trapped the 370 Greek triremes in the Megarian Channel. The Greeks retreated northward, luring the Persians into the narrow waters near Salamis. Once there, the Persian fleet could not maneuver. The Greeks turned and went on the attack. They sank 300 Persian galleys and lost only 40 ships of their own.

Key Dates

- 480 BCE Battle of Salamis. Greeks beat Persians.

- 31 BCE Battle of Actium. Caesar Octavian defeats Mark Antony in Roman Civil War.

- CE 1340 Battle of Sluys between French and English as part of 100 Years War. Warships become battlefields.

- 1571 Battle of Lepanto. Austrians beat Turks.

- 1588 England defeats Spanish Armada.

Sail or Oar?

IN THE ANCIENT WORLD, trading ships used sails and wind power to move around the seas. Captains of warships could not rely on winds and tide alone. They used manpower as well. Greek, Roman, Turkish and Spanish ships used massed oarsmen. Others, such as the Anglo-Saxons, Norsemen and Normans, used a combination of sail and oars. The French and British preferred sail-powered vessels and improved their design through the centuries.

The Greeks were first with the oar-driven warship. They used vessels called triremes, which had three rows of oars and 150 rowers. Athenian sailors developed a way of fighting using their rowing skills. They would approach an enemy ship at full speed, come alongside and at the last minute pull in their oars. This smashed all the oars on the enemy ship, which were still sticking out.

▲ THE MARY ROSE
Henry VIII's flag ship was armed with cannons low down which could fire broadsides.

◄ ARMED GALLEY
A Roman sculpture shows the banks of oars with armed soldiers at the ready on deck.

▲ GALLEY SLAVES
Chained to their benches in the dark, hot smelly hull of their boat, galley slaves could be worked until they died. Their bodies would be thrown over the side.

A HARD LIFE
Few people wanted to row a galley. Criminals in countries such as Italy or Spain in the 15th and 16th centuries were often condemned to the galleys as a punishment. Prisoners of war were also made to row in their enemy's galleys.

▶ OARS AT WORK
There were three layers of galley slaves in a trireme. To be effective they had to be able to row in time, so a drum was used to beat out the rhythm.

◄ MEDITERRANEAN GALLEY
Fast, light, unarmed boats were used to transport troops. If the boat was sunk in battle, the soldiers and the rowers were picked up by their own side and the boat was abandoned.

▸ FLOATING BATTLES
Spanish and English ships engage in battle in 1372 as part of the 100 Years War. The warships sailed very close together, and the soldiers fought across the decks as if on land.

The oarsmen in the galleys were normally slaves. Some were convicted criminals, but many were prisoners of war. By the time of the Battle of Lepanto (1571), the Turks had smaller galleys called galiots with 18 to 24 oars, and the Venetians had developed a large vessel called a galleas. Galleys were equipped with sails so that with favorable winds they could operate without using the oarsmen.

The Scandinavian raiders who roamed as far away as the Mediterranean and Black Sea used both wind and manpower. Under Bjarni Herjolfsson, a Viking longboat reached North America in 985 CE. The Vikings could row their long, narrow boats when there was no wind or they were close inshore. Because the vessels were light and almost flat on the bottom, they could land on gently shelving coasts or even mud flats.

By the 14th and 15th century, all warships in northern Europe relied on wind power. The sailors working in the tidal, stormy waters of the English Channel and North Sea needed to be very skillful.

Under Henry VIII, ship design began to change. By the time of the Armada, British warships were sleek and low. They were about 38 yards (35 m) long and 11 yards (10 m) wide and were called galleons. Like the galley, they were ships built specially for war. New designs in sails and rigging made the vessels even more seaworthy. The galleon was able to make long distance voyages, and so it became the vessel used by navigators and explorers.

▲ FAST AND FURIOUS
Vikings used their fast boats to make lightning raids. They were able to sail as far as America. The chance of plunder and easy pickings made the risky journey worthwhile.

Viking war-rior

Key Dates

- 241 BCE Lilybaeum. After a long siege, Rome defeats Carthage, and Carthaginians lose 120 ships.

- CE 655 Battle of the Masts. Moaviah governor of Syria attempts to capture Constantinople from the sea.

- 841 Vikings reach Dublin.

- 1027 Normans land near Naples and establish stronghold.

- 1281 Mongol invasion of Japan defeated by "divine wind" or "kamikaze."

- 1588 Spanish Armada in running battles with the English fleet along the south coast of England.

Ramming and Grappling

Before gunpowder allowed ships to stand off at a distance and bombard one another, warships used light siege weapons, archers and slingers. The siege weapons could kill and injure people and damage sails and rigging. The archers and slingers acted as snipers, picking out targets on the enemy ships.

Ramming could cause major damage. From the Greeks in 600 BCE to the Spanish Armada of 1588, galleys powered by oars were fitted with a long ramming beak. The trick was to drive this into the hull of the enemy ship.

▲ GREEK FIRE
Fire can be used as a weapon at sea. "Greek fire," a flammable chemical, was used by Byzantine ships around the 4th century.

The Romans introduced a new weapon in 260 BCE at the Battle of Mylae in Sicily. The corvus or "crow" was a hinged gangplank with a weighted hook. It could be swung out over an enemy ship and dropped so that it was stuck in the deck. Then a boarding party raced across the corvus on to the enemy ship. The Romans won at Mylae and took control of the Mediterranean.

Grappling irons, hooks with heavy chains, were later used in sea battles to assist boarding. Once the ships were alongside and the boarding parties in action, the fight became a land battle at sea, with hand-to-hand combat. Medieval ships showed this in their design with crenellated wooden "castles" in the bow and stern.

▲ SHIP RAM
This massive bronze-cased ram could easily pierce the hull of an enemy ship if it struck broadside.

WAR AT SEA
Before gunpowder changed war, ships could ram the enemy, or slice off their oars. Other weapons were the corvus and twin-hulled siege vessels which could carry fighting towers.

◀ DECORATIVE RAM
This finely worked prow with its ram shaped like a row of swords shows the quality of the work on classical warships.

▲ ROMAN SEA BATTLE
Some sea battles between the Romans and Carthaginians were on a huge scale, with ships locked together as boarding parties fought.

▲ FIRE SHIP
This ingenious little ship is designed to carry a tub of burning tar into the middle of an enemy fleet at anchor. It could damage rigging and sails and had the potential to sink ships much larger than itself. The English sent fire ships like this one against the Spanish Armada when it was at anchor.

▶ CROWS AND TOWERS
The Romans developed a grappling weapon called a corvus, the Latin word for crow. It looked rather like a crow's big beak. It was a hinged gangplank with a hook which sank into the enemy ship's deck. Special twin-hulled siege vessels could carry fighting towers to the enemy.

Corvus   Siege tower   Twin-hulled ship

Roman warship

Spike

This is why the front of a ship is known as the forecastle or fo'c'sle.

The English warship the Mary Rose, lost off Portsmouth in 1545, marks the change from ancient to modern warfare at sea. When she was recovered in 1982 from the mud into which she had settled, her weapons included both longbows and cannons. The ship was designed without castles but with gun ports on the lower decks. Heavy broadside cannons stood on these gun decks. When they opened fire, their shot would damage the hulls and masts of enemy ships.

In the running battle with the Spanish Armada in 1588, the English Royal Navy demonstrated that modern ship design, skilled sailors and good weather could shift the odds in favor of a smaller force. The Spanish had 20 great galleons, 44 armed merchant ships, 23 transports, 35 smaller vessels, four galleases (a double sized heavily armed galley) and four galleys. The warships mounted a total of 2,431 guns. The English had 68 ships in Plymouth, a London squadron of 30 ships and a further squadron of 23 in the eastern English Channel. Aside from seafaring skills and ship design, their strength lay in their 1,800 heavy cannons, mostly long-range cannons called culverins.

In running battles up the Channel the English finally prevented the Spanish from landing in England.

◀ ARMADA
Before dawn on July 28, 1588, the English sent fire ships into the Spanish fleet off Flanders as part of their running battle with the Armada. It forced the Spanish to cut their anchor cables. In the great sea battle that followed, only a storm prevented the English fleet from capturing or destroying 16 of the most damaged Spanish ships.

Key Dates

- 480 BCE Battle of Salamis, Greece. Greeks defeat Persians.

- 262 BCE Battle of Mylae, Sicily. Romans win and take control of the Mediterranean Sea.

- 241 BCE Battle of Lilybaeum, Sicily. Romans defeat the Carthaginians.

- 31 BCE Battle of Actium, Greece. Romans defeat Cleopatra and the Egyptians.

- CE 1571 Battle of Lepanto. Christian Allies defeat Turks.

- 1588 Defeat of the Spanish Armada by the English.

Sailing to War

CARRYING SOLDIERS AND THEIR WEAPONS, vehicles, horses and food by sea and landing them on an enemy shore is called an amphibious operation. Amphibious means able to work on land and in water. In ancient times, this was a simple operation. Coasts weren't always defended and boats were flat enough to land directly on sand or shingle shores.

As ships became bigger, they had to remain off shore and troops transferred to smaller boats before they could land. Horses could swim ashore on their own, but artillery and wagons posed an extra problem. In bad weather these operations could be dangerous, and so sailors and soldiers looked for sheltered anchorages where they could land and unload in safety.

One of the earliest recorded amphibious operations was the Punic Wars of 264–241 BCE between the Carthaginians, who lived in what is now Tunisia, and the Romans, in modern Italy. Both sides transported men and horses across the Mediterranean. The Carthaginian general Hannibal even took about 80 war elephants by ship from North Africa into Spain.

There were earlier operations. The most famous is described in Homer's *Iliad*, an epic poem that includes both myth and fact. To lay siege to Troy (a city located in what is now Turkey) the Greeks, under Agamemnon, had to sail across the Aegean Sea. Archaeological evidence of both Troy and the Trojan Wars dates the sea crossing to around 1200 BCE.

At Marathon, in September 490 BCE a Persian invasion fleet landed a force of 20,000 on the Greek

BATTLES BY LAND AND SEA

Islands could not be attacked without the use of ships. Sometimes the landings were the beginning of a long campaign. They could be part of the siege of a fortified port, or the means of escape for a battle fought on the coast. Vikings used their boats like a modern "getaway car," raiding a settlement and escaping quickly.

▲ NATURAL LIFT
A Sumerian warrior uses an inflated animal skin as a float to help him to cross a fast-flowing river.

▲ HELEN OF TROY
The wife of the king of Sparta was so beautiful that her face was said to have "launched a thousand ships." She was kidnapped by Paris of Troy, which began the Trojan Wars.

◀ TROOP CARRIERS
Boats like this one were used to ferry troops across the Mediterranean to fight battles on land.

coast near Athens. They were defeated by the Athenians, who numbered only 11,000, but despite heavy losses, they were able to reach their ships and escape.

In Europe there was usually no need for soldiers to travel by sea. The waves of raids by the sea-going Saxons between 205 CE and 577 and the Viking raids between 800–1016 reached eastern England and northern France. They were not so much amphibious operations as military "smash and grab raids." The Anglo-Saxons and the Vikings eventually settled in the territories they had been raiding.

For island countries, such as Britain, that might be threatened by enemy landings, it was a good idea to build watchtowers and fortifications at the harbors and likely landing sites.

▲ THE NEW WORLD
In the 16th century, Spanish and Portuguese explorers sailed west and invaded large areas of South America.

▼ INVASION
In 1066, William of Normandy transported 9,000 men with all their horses and equipment for his invasion of England.

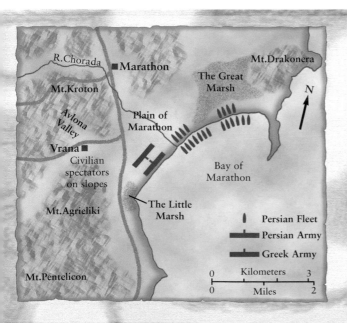

◄ THE BATTLE OF MARATHON
In 490 BCE Persia invaded Greece. The Persian leader Darius worked his way down from modern-day Turkey in the north, with a force of 150,000 men in ships. He landed an army 20,000 strong near Marathon. The Greeks met them on the coastal plain with about 11,000 soldiers and lost only 192 to the Persians' 6,400.

Key Dates

- 490 BCE Battle of Marathon. The Greeks defeat the Persians.

- 415 BCE Athenians land in Sicily and besiege Syracuse.

- 54 BCE First Roman invasion of Britain.

- CE 43 Second Roman invasion of Britain.

- 400s Raids on England by Jutes, Angles and Saxons.

- 700s–800s Vikings raid Europe.

- 1027 Normans land in southern Italy.

- 1066 Normans invade England.

Glossary

A

arquebus Muzzle-loading gunpowder weapon fired from the shoulder or supported on a tripod.

artillery In an army, large weapons that need transport to move them around the battlefield and a crew of soldiers to use them.

B

bayonet A blade fitted onto the end of a musket, named after the French town of Bayonne.

broadside The side of a ship that can be seen above the waterline.

butt The end of a gun stock, which is placed against the shoulder when the gun is being fired.

C

crusades A series of campaigns led by Christian knights to regain the Holy Land (the area around Jerusalem) from the Muslims.

creese
Malay dagger with a distinctive wavy blade.

cuirass Armor for the front and back of the upper body, originally made from leather.

cuisse Armor for protecting the front of the thigh.

E

emplacement The position of an artillery gun on the battlefield or outside a besieged castle.

English Civil War Conflict between Royalists, under Charles I, and Republicans under Oliver Cromwell. It lasted from 1642 to 1649, when the king was executed. Cromwell ruled until 1669 when Charles II came to the throne.

G

gisarme Medieval weapon based on a French weeding tool.

glaive Halberd with a blade that looks like a sword.

H

hand-and-a-half Heavy sword that could not be used easily with only one hand but was not quite as large as a two-handed sword.

hoplite An infantry soldier from ancient Greece who was heavily armed. Hoplon is the Greek word for tool or weapon.

I

infantry The soldiers who fight on foot with hand-held weapons. The infantry usually forms the largest part of any army.

J

jousting Sporting combat between two knights on horseback, fighting with blunt weapons. Jousts were often social gatherings.

K

knuckle duster Slang word for a metal weapon worn on the hand over the knuckles. It gives extra power to a punch in a fist fight.

L

legionary Roman soldiers were called legionaries because they belonged to a legion. Legions were the main units of the Roman army. A legion contained between 3,000 and 6,000 infantry soldiers, plus a cavalry unit.

linstock The stick or pole used to hold a length of slow burning cord that has been soaked in saltpeter, used to ignite the gunpowder.

M

medieval Term describing people, events and objects from the time known as the Middle Ages.

Middle Ages Period in history generally agreed to have lasted from around 800 CE to 1400.

miguelet A Spanish flintlock firearm that has a mainspring and hammer on the outside. It was also known as a miquelet.

Mongol Word used to describe the people, events and objects of the Mongolian tribes who invaded Europe after the fall of the Roman Empire in the mid 500s.

musket A firearm that was loaded at the muzzle and had a smooth bore.

N

Norman Conquest The name given to the defeat of England by the Normans. William Duke of Normandy successfully invaded England in 1066, seized the throne and was crowned King William I on Christmas Day.

P

parry To turn aside a sword thrust from an opponent.

pauldron Piece of armor made to cover the shoulder.

pistol Firearm designed to be used with one hand. It has a short stock, or handle, and barrel.

poleyn Piece of armor made to protect the knee.

pommel The weighted end of the handle of a broad sword, used to deliver a hammer blow in battle.

Punic Wars Three wars that were fought between Rome and Carthage over the territories of the Mediterranean region.

R

rampart Wide earth mound built to fortify a castle or town. It usually had a parapet on top.

S

saltpeter A mineral known as potassium nitrate. It is used to make gunpowder, explosives, matches and fertilizers.

Samurai A word first used to describe the imperial guard of ancient Japan. Later it was used to describe the warrior class in general. Warriors could only be Samurai by birth.

snaphaunce A firearm with a snap or spring lock.

Spanish Armada An armada is a fleet of battle ships. The Spanish armada was a fleet sent by Philip of Spain that tried to invade England in 1588 but was not successful. The fight was about Spain's rich territories in southern America.

Spartan Word describing people, events and objects from Sparta, a city state of ancient Greece.

squire A trainee knight aged about 14. He carried the shield and equipment of his instructor, attended to his horse, and defended him in battle. He was taught courtly as well as military skills.

stock The wooden grip or handle of a firearm.

Stone Age Period before the Bronze Age (around 5,000 years ago) when stones and flints were used to make tools and weapons.

Swiss Guard Group of Swiss soldiers chosen to guard the Pope. The tradition was begun by Pope Julius II in the early 1500s. Today, a Papal Swiss Guard is still used to guard the Pope.

T

tournament Armed contest between medieval knights, fought for honor and ceremony.

trident Fork with three prongs.

trireme War ship used by ancient Greeks. Its name comes from the Greek word for "three" and "oar," because it was driven by men rowing three ranks of oars.

For More Information

Allegheny Arms and Armor Museum
505-1/2 West Main Street
Smethport, PA 16749
(814) 887-0947
Web site: http://www.armormuseum.com
Educational museum that preserves military vehicles, armor, weapons, and more.

British Museum
Great Russell Street
London, UK
WC1B 3DG
Web site: http://www.britishmuseum.org
Founded in 1783, the first national public museum in the world.

Higgins Armory Museum
100 Barber Avenus
Worchester, MA 01606-2444
(508) 853-6015
Web site: http://www.higgins.org
Museum with a large collection of arms and armor ranging from ancient Greece to the height of the Renaissance.

Japanese Sword Society of the United States
Box 712
Breckenridge, TX 76024
(817) 559-5532
Web site: http://www.jssus.org
An educational organization for the appreciation and study of the Japanese sword.

The Metropolitan Museum of Art
1000 Fifth Avenue
New York, NY 10028-0198
(212) 535-7710
Web site: http://www.metmuseum.org
Founded in 1870, one of the largest art museums in the world, with more than two million works of art spanning five thousand years of world culture.

National Infantry Museum and Soldier Center
1775 Legacy Way
Columbus, GA 31903
(706) 685-5800
Web site: http://www.nationalinfantrymuseum.com
American museum dedicated to infantrymen from the past and present, with over 30,000 artifacts.

Smithsonian Institution
National Museum of American History
Department of the History of Science and Technology
Division of Armed Forces History
AHB 4013, MRC 620
Washington, DC 20560
(202) 357-1883
Web site: http://americanhistory.si.edu
Large collection of firearms at the Smithsonian Institution.

Web Sites

Due to the changing nature of Internet links, Rosen Publishing has developed an online list of Web sites related to the subject of this book. This site is updated regularly. Please use this link to access the list:

http://www.rosenlinks.com/jth/weap

For Further Reading

Alexander, Caroline. *The War That Killed Achilles: The True Story of Homer's Iliad and the Trojan War.* New York: Penguin, 2009.

Boos, Ben. *Swords: An Artist's Devotion.* Cambridge, MA: Candlewick, 2008.

Byam, Michele. *Arms and Armor.* New York: DK, 2004.

Castle and Knight. New York: DK, 2006.

Homer and W.H.D. Rouse (trans.) *The Iliad.* New York: Penguin, 2007.

Kelly, Jack. *Gunpowder: Alchemy, Bombards, and Pyrotechnics: The History of the Explosive That Changed the World.* New York: Basic Books, 2005.

Louis, Thomas and Tommy Ito. *Samurai: The Code of the Warrior.* New York: Sterling, 2008.

Murrell, Deborah. *Weapons.* New York: Gareth Stevens, 2008.

Nossov, Konstantin. *Ancient and Medieval Siege Weapons: A Fully Illustrated Guide to Siege Weapons and Tactics.* Guilford, CT: Lyons Press, 2005.

Sidnell, Philip. *Warhorse: Cavalry in the Ancient World.* London: Continuum International, 2006.

Soar, Hugh D.H. *The Crooked Stick: A History of the Longbow.* Yardley, PA: Westholme, 2009.

Sun-tzu. *The Art of War.* Boston, MA: Shambhala Publications, 2005.

Thompson, Logan. *Ancient Weapons in Britain.* Barnsley, UK: Pen and Sword, 2005.

War: From Bronze-Age Battles to 21st Century Conflict. New York: DK, 2009.

Weapon: A Visual History of Arms and Armor. New York: DK, 2006.

Index

About the Author

Will Fowler is a consultant and writer specializing in defense, current affairs and military history. He is a recognized authority on many aspects of history and military equipment and regularly broadcasts on radio and television. He is the author of over 30 books covering military technology and conflicts from the 19th century to the Second Gulf War. He enjoys making his in-depth knowledge of military history accessible to young readers.